Little Boys Bible Storybook

Little Boys Bible Storybook

Carolyn Larsen
Illustrated by Caron Turk

BakerBooks
Grand Rapids, Michigan

Published by Baker Books
a division of Baker Publishing Group
P.O. Box 6287, Grand Rapids, MI 49516-6287
www.bakerbooks.com

Previously published as two books: *Little Boys Bible Storybook for Mothers &
Sons* (© 1999) and *Little Boys Bible Storybook for Fathers & Sons* (© 2001)

Printed in China

Library of Congress Cataloging-in-Publication Data
Larsen, Carolyn, 1950–
    Little boys Bible storybook / Carolyn Larsen ; Illustrated by Caron Turk.
        p.   cm.
    "Previously published as two books: Little boys Bible storybook for
mothers & sons (1999) and Little boys Bible storybook for fathers & sons
(2001)"—ECIP galley.
    ISBN 10: 0-8010-4533-9 (cloth)
    ISBN 978-0-8010-4533-2 (cloth)
    1. Bible stories, English. 2. Mothers and sons—Religious aspects—
Christianity—Juvenile literature. 3. Fathers and sons—Religious aspects—
Christianity—Juvenile literature. I. Turk, Caron. II. Title.
BS551.3.L3695 2007
220.9′505—dc22   2007007979

Contents

Part 2: Stories for Fathers and Sons

Part 1

Stories for Mothers and Sons

Dear Moms,

I had two daughters before my son was born. I remember people saying, "Boys are so different from girls, you'll see!" I didn't believe them because one of my daughters was an absolute daredevil and I didn't see how a boy could be any more energetic than she was. However, they were right. It's hard to explain how—but boys are definitely different to raise than girls are. That's why Caron Turk and I have tried to make this book a little more active, maybe a little more "rough-and-tumble" than the *Little Girls Bible Storybook.*

We hope the stories and illustrations in this book provide a chance for you and your son to see into the hearts of some well-loved Bible characters. Of course, we don't really know what those people actually felt or how they approached some of the situations they were in, but by thinking about what they may have felt, we can understand some of the lessons they learned from their experiences. We hope this book helps your son realize that these were real people with problems, joys, successes and failures—people like us!

Caron has created a spunky little boy angel who is hiding in every illustration. Often his buddy, a little daredevil lizard, is with him. You and your son will have fun looking for the two of them.

My hope is that this book will bring familiar Bible stories to life for you and your son, and that the questions and thoughts in the Becoming a Man of God section will be good conversation starters for the two of you. I'm sure your son will love hearing about your childhood memories and experiences.

God bless you and your son as you read the *Little Boys Bible Storybook*.

Carolyn Larsen

That's What Little Boys Are Made Of

A big, goofy-looking brown bear scooped honey into his mouth as fast as he could shovel it. When the earth under his feet began to shake, the bear dove behind a rock, peeking out at the swirling dust. The bear didn't know it, but God himself was moving the dirt! He was shaping it into his last and best creation—Adam, the very first man.

Adam stretched his arms and wiggled his fingers—everything worked! He jumped up and raced through the garden, checking out everything God had made for him. He skipped stones across a lake. He climbed a tree and hung upside down. What fun Adam had!

But, just a little while later Adam slumped on the ground, pulling blades of grass and tossing them into a stream. "What's the matter, son?" God asked.

"I don't know. I guess I'm bored." Adam sighed.

"Hmmm, well, would you like to name the animals?" God asked, trying to think of something fun. "They all need names, and you can decide what to call each one. Maybe you'll find one to be your buddy." So God marched the animals by, and Adam made up names for each one. But when he finished, he plopped down on the ground again.

"I know what the problem is," God whispered. "You're lonely!"

"I'm what?"

"Lonely. You need someone to talk with and do things with. Someone who is more like you than the animals are." God made Adam fall asleep, and he took one of Adam's ribs and used it to make Eve, the first woman.

You will be best friends..... ♥

"Wake up now, my son," God whispered. Adam opened his eyes and saw a brand-new, beautiful creature. "This is Eve," God said. "I made her to be your friend and your wife. You both are a lot like me—you can think, and talk, make decisions, and work together. I know you'll be very happy!"

Based on Genesis 1–2

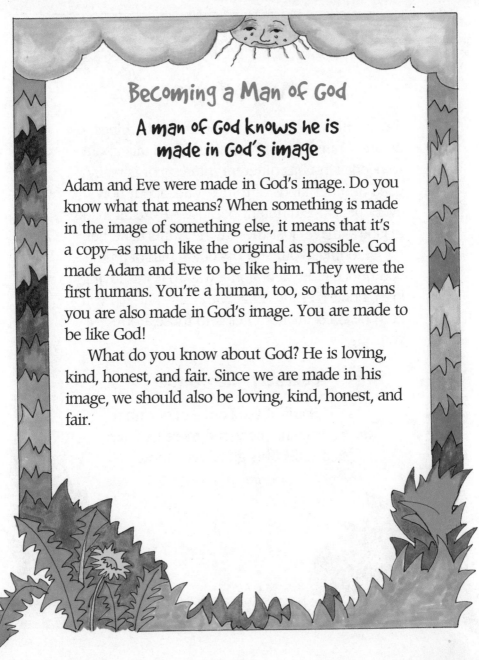

Becoming a Man of God

A man of God knows he is made in God's image

Adam and Eve were made in God's image. Do you know what that means? When something is made in the image of something else, it means that it's a copy—as much like the original as possible. God made Adam and Eve to be like him. They were the first humans. You're a human, too, so that means you are also made in God's image. You are made to be like God!

What do you know about God? He is loving, kind, honest, and fair. Since we are made in his image, we should also be loving, kind, honest, and fair.

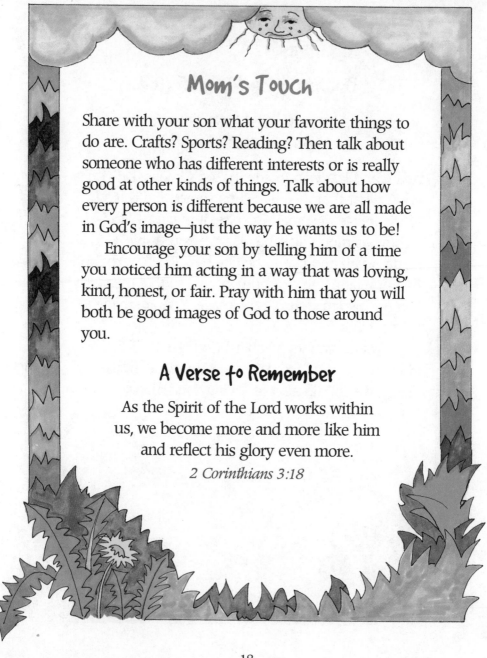

Mom's Touch

Share with your son what your favorite things to do are. Crafts? Sports? Reading? Then talk about someone who has different interests or is really good at other kinds of things. Talk about how every person is different because we are all made in God's image—just the way he wants us to be!

Encourage your son by telling him of a time you noticed him acting in a way that was loving, kind, honest, or fair. Pray with him that you will both be good images of God to those around you.

A Verse to Remember

As the Spirit of the Lord works within us, we become more and more like him and reflect his glory even more.

2 Corinthians 3:18

At First B🍎te

"Adam! Adam!" Eve's excited voice blasted through the quiet garden. Adam could hear her running, pushing aside branches, and stumbling over bushes.

"Over here, Eve," he called. He stepped out from behind a bush just in time for Eve to crash into him. "Ugh! What's wrong?" he moaned as he picked himself up from the ground.

"Taste this—it's great!" Eve cried, shoving a half-eaten piece of fruit in his face. Thick, golden juice ran down her arm, dripping into a little puddle on the ground.

Adam's breath caught in his throat. His stomach twisted into a ball of fear. "Th-th-th-that's from the tree God said not to eat from, Eve. He said if we eat from it we'll die."

Adam recognized the fruit because he had spent lots of time walking around that tree, looking at the fruit, wondering if it was juicy, wondering why God didn't want him to eat it. Drops of sweat popped out on his forehead because Eve had broken the only rule God gave them.

"Oh phooey, we won't die. That snake over there said that this fruit would make us more like God," Eve whined. "Come on, taste it. I promise you'll thank me."

Adam knew he should just walk away, and that's what
he wanted to do. But, Eve held the fruit right under his
nose and it smelled so sweet and the juice ran down
her arm . . . suddenly he grabbed it and stuffed it in his
mouth. "M-m-m-m, good," he mumbled. Then a pain shot
through his heart as Adam realized he had also broken
God's rule.

When God came to the garden later, Adam hid from him. Right away God knew something was wrong. "Oh, Adam, what have you done?"

"Well . . . I . . . the snake . . ." Adam tried to pass the blame. Finally he blurted out, "It's Eve's fault!"

"Yeah, but . . ." Eve started to argue, but when Adam touched her arm she stopped. There was no way out of this. They had disobeyed and that was that.

"I have to punish you," God said sadly, "but remember that I still love you. I will always love you."

Based on Genesis 3

Becoming a Man of God

A man of God takes responsibility for his sin

Adam and Eve were made in God's image. But they didn't have to always do what he wanted them to do. They could choose to obey or not to obey. In this story, they made a bad choice—they sinned—and God punished them. Sometimes the only way we learn lessons is through punishment. That's not much fun, is it? But we remember the lessons we learn when we've been punished.

Everybody sins—even if we try hard not to, we do. When was a time that you did something wrong? Were you punished? How?

Mom's Touch

OK, Mom, it's important for your son to know that you sometimes sin. Tell him about a time when you did something wrong. Were you punished? How did you handle that punishment?

Reinforce to your son that everybody makes mistakes and bad choices. When we do, we should admit it and accept the punishment that is given. We can learn from our mistakes and hopefully not make the same mistake over and over. Remind your son that God loves him no matter what—and so do you!

A Verse to Remember

No matter how deep the stain of your sins, I can remove it. I can make you as clean as freshly fallen snow.

Isaiah 1:18

TATTLETALE

"Why don't you get a real job? How hard can it be to follow a bunch of sissy sheep around?" Cain sneered. Abel just shook his head and went back to watching his sheep.

It seemed to Eve that her boys fought about everything. Actually Cain fought about everything—for some deep-inside-his-heart reason he always tried to prove he was better, stronger, or smarter than his younger brother. She hoped he would outgrow it, but as he got older Cain's jealousy got worse.

One afternoon Cain was working in his fields when he noticed his brother building an altar. "Oh great, that goody-two-shoes is giving an offering to God. Guess that means I have to give one, too. Well, I'm not about to burn up my best grain. I'll just use this scraggly stuff. No one will know anyway."

Cain and Abel each gave their offering to God. But to Cain's surprise God accepted Abel's offering, but rejected his. "WHAT? NO FAIR! NO FAIR!!" Cain shouted. He stomped across the field, kicking down his best grain and mashing it flat.

"Cain, what are you so upset about?" God asked. "Give your offering in the right way and I will accept it, too. Watch it, you're letting sin into your heart!"

The next day Cain was still boiling mad! He came up with a dirty plan. "Hey, bro, I'm sorry I got so mad yesterday," he said sweetly. "Look, I need some help in my field; will you give me a hand?"

"Sure, glad to help," Abel said, with a brotherly slap on Cain's back. But when they got to the field; Cain grabbed a stick and whopped Abel on the head. "Take that, you lousy do-gooder!" Abel fell down—dead.

No one saw Cain kill Abel so he jogged home, thinking he had gotten away with murder. Then God asked him, "Cain, where is your brother, Abel?"

"How should I know? It's not my job to know where he is every minute," Cain snapped.

"Abel's blood cries out to me from the ground," God said quietly. "You're guilty of murder. Your punishment is that you must leave your home and wander the earth for the rest of your life!"

Based on Genesis 4:1-12

Becoming a Man of God
A man of God gives God his best

Does this story sound like God was playing favorites by choosing Abel over Cain? It can sound that way until you look a little deeper. Cain didn't give God the best of his grain. Even worse than that—he didn't give God the best of his heart. He gave an offering only because he saw Abel giving one—not because he was thankful to God or wanted to worship him. Then, he gave God leftovers, not the best of what he had. God wants the best of our love, worship, service, and gifts.

In what ways do you worship God? How can you give him the best of what you have?

Mom's Touch

Your children will learn how important proper worship is by watching how you worship. Talk with your son about what it means to give God your best. Talk about ways to give him the best of your money, time, worship, and praise. Explain to your son how you do this.

Pray with your son that you both can have the right attitudes about worshiping God and giving him your best, not just time and money that is left over from your life.

A Verse to Remember

Great is the LORD! He is most worthy of praise! He is to be revered above all the gods.

Psalm 96:4

Dad's Little Helpers

"Boys, get up! Dad needs your help." Shem, Ham, and Japheth slowly sat up and rubbed the sleep from their eyes.

"Why does he need our help so early?" Shem muttered.

"Shh. Don't start the day by complaining," said his mother. "Your breakfast is already on the table."

The boys sat down to eat, not very happy to be awake. Their mother smiled and gently reminded them, "Remember, we're all helping your father build the ark because God told him to build it. We're obeying God."

Just then Noah came in. "That's right, boys. God is tired of the way people are behaving. Everyone is selfish and mean. No one pays any attention to God anymore."

"Yeah, so God is going to wipe out the whole world with a big flood," Ham shouted. He stood on his chair and jumped off, pretending to be drowning.

"This is not a joke, Ham," his mother said sternly. "Everyone is going to die . . . except us. That's because your father has led our family to honor and obey God. We have a lot of work to do. Finish your breakfasts."

Soon the whole family was out in the yard. Each boy had a job to do. Shem brought the wood, Ham carried buckets of tar, and little Japheth smeared the tar on the boards.

Day after day, week after week, year after year the little family worked. By the time the ark was finished, the boys were grown up and married. Their whole lives they had worked on the ark with their father.

One day after the ark was finished, Japheth came running into the house. "Father, there's hundreds of animals headed this way—hundreds! What do we do?"

"Open the ark. Let them in," Noah answered.

"Grab that food, boys," Mrs. Noah called, "and get your wives. We're going for a boat ride!" The Noah family followed the animals into the ark and God himself closed the big door. Just then rain began to fall.

Based on Genesis 6:1–7:9

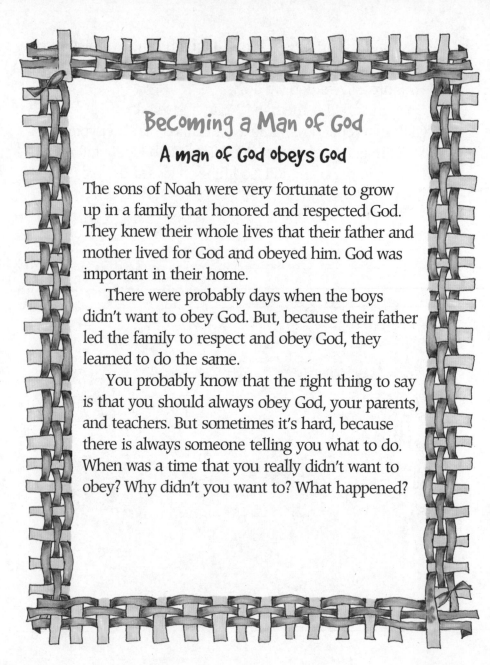

Becoming a Man of God
A man of God obeys God

The sons of Noah were very fortunate to grow up in a family that honored and respected God. They knew their whole lives that their father and mother lived for God and obeyed him. God was important in their home.

There were probably days when the boys didn't want to obey God. But, because their father led the family to respect and obey God, they learned to do the same.

You probably know that the right thing to say is that you should always obey God, your parents, and teachers. But sometimes it's hard, because there is always someone telling you what to do. When was a time that you really didn't want to obey? Why didn't you want to? What happened?

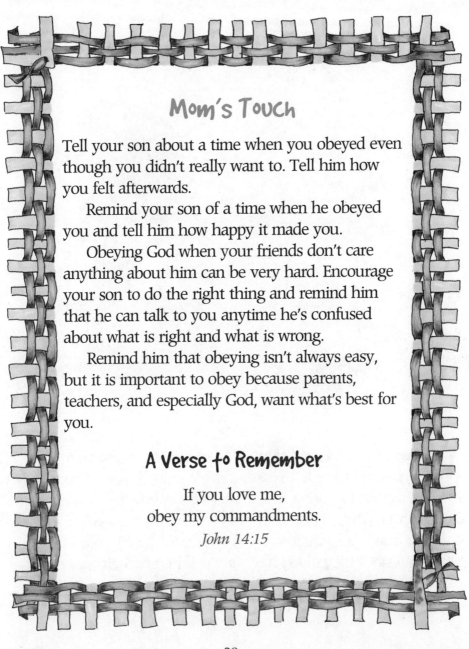

Mom's Touch

Tell your son about a time when you obeyed even though you didn't really want to. Tell him how you felt afterwards.

Remind your son of a time when he obeyed you and tell him how happy it made you.

Obeying God when your friends don't care anything about him can be very hard. Encourage your son to do the right thing and remind him that he can talk to you anytime he's confused about what is right and what is wrong.

Remind him that obeying isn't always easy, but it is important to obey because parents, teachers, and especially God, want what's best for you.

A Verse to Remember

If you love me,
obey my commandments.
John 14:15

The Miracle Baby

Whew, it's hot today! Abraham thought, sitting down in the shade of the only tree around. He fanned himself and listened to Sarah working inside their tent. A little heat didn't stop Sarah from making dinner and even stirring up a few treats for the children who were sure to drop by later. Kids loved Abraham and Sarah and since they didn't have any children of their own they had plenty of time to spend with their nieces and nephews.

Abraham looked up at the waves of heat rising from the desert sand. "That can't be someone walking across the desert in this heat. I must be seeing things." Abraham rubbed his eyes and looked again. Soon he could make out three men coming toward him. "Hey," he called. "Come over here in the shade. Sit down and rest for a while!"

"Sarah, bring some water and some food for our guests," Abraham called. As the men ate Sarah's dinner and drank the cool water they talked. "We'll come back at about this time next year," one man said. "By then, Sarah will be the proud mother of a baby boy." This was amazing news since Abraham and Sarah were both very old—too old to have a baby, that's for sure!

Sarah was listening from inside the tent and when she heard
what the man said, a quick "harumpff" slipped out before she
could slap a hand over her mouth. She looked at her wrinkled
hands, fingers bent from arthritis, and it suddenly struck
her funny to think that her old body could have a baby. She
started laughing and didn't stop until tears were spilling down
her wrinkled cheeks.

"Why did Sarah laugh?" the stranger asked Abraham. "Does she think this is too hard for God?" Poor old Abraham was in shock himself at the news of becoming a father after all these years. He didn't know what to think. The men left then, but sure enough nearly a year later, Sarah and Abraham were counting the fingers and toes of their newborn son, Isaac.

Based on Genesis 18:1-15; 21:1-7

Becoming a Man of God
A man of God believes God

Abraham and Sarah tried to always obey God. They trusted him and did whatever he asked them to do, even when what he asked was hard.

They had always wanted a child, but they were both so old now that it seemed impossible. When the man said that Sarah was going to have a baby, Sarah wasn't quite sure at first, but she quickly believed him because when God says he's going to do something, that settles it!

Being able to believe what someone tells you is so important. Has someone ever told you he would do something and then not done it? How did you feel? Did you believe that person the next time he told you he would do something?

Mom's Touch

Share a story about a time when someone disappointed you by not keeping his word. Talk about how hard it was to believe that person the next time.

We can always believe God's promises. How do we know what his promises are? By reading his Word and understanding it.

Help your son understand that sometimes we have to wait a long time for God to do what he says, but that's OK, because we know that if he said he will do something—he will!

A Verse to Remember

Without wavering, let us hold tightly to
the hope we say we have, for God can
be trusted to keep his promise.

Hebrews 10:23

No More Teasing!

I saac was Sarah's pride and joy. After all, she had waited a long time for this child. When Isaac was still a little guy his father, Abraham, threw a party for him. Everyone ate and played games. Isaac was the center of attention and enjoying it very much—until his stepbrother Ishmael began teasing him—holding a cookie just out of Isaac's reach and whining, "Come on, little baby—take it. Why don't you take it, you baby?"

Sarah watched Ishmael's mean game. She heard Isaac's cries, and she got more and more angry. Finally, she threw down the plate she was holding and stomped across the yard to Abraham. "I want that bully out of here. Send Ishmael and his mother away. That boy will not have any part of your inheritance! It all belongs to Isaac!"

Abraham sadly told Ishmael's mother, Hagar, that she and Ishmael had to leave. "No, please don't send us away! I won't tease Isaac anymore. I promise!" Ishmael cried. He didn't want to leave his home and his dad. Abraham didn't want his son to leave, either. But he felt better when God told him not to worry because he would take care of Ishmael and Hagar. God even told him that Ishmael would be the leader of a nation when he grew up.

Abraham gave them water, hugged his son, and sent Hagar and Ishmael away. They wandered around in the wilderness for a long time.

When their food and water were gone, Ishmael cried, "I'm thirsty. I want to go home." He got so weak that Hagar was afraid he would die. With tears rolling down her cheeks, she walked away from him and prayed, "God, I can't take it. My son is dying!"

She was crying so hard that she didn't even notice the angel God sent to comfort her. "Hagar," the angel said, "it's OK. God heard Ishmael's cries. He wants you to know that your son will be fine." Hagar opened her eyes and saw a well, filled to the brim with cool, clear water. She got a drink for Ishmael and hugged him tightly. Love spilled from her heart as she thanked God for his care.

Based on Genesis 21:8-21

Becoming a Man of God

A man of God knows
God will take care of him

Hagar was scared because she thought her son was going to die. Ishmael's father, Abraham, turned his back on them, so she had no place left to turn, except to God.

Actually, while Hagar may have felt that she was at the end of her rope—she was really in the best possible place. God loves his children and loves to take care of them. So, we can talk to him about whatever we need and he will help us.

What are some ways that God takes care of you?

Mom's Touch

This is a good opportunity to share some things that concern you. It's healthy for your son to know that adults have worries and concerns, but that you talk to God about them and believe that he will take care of you. Tell him about a specific time when you talked to God about a problem and he took care of you in a special way.

Make a list of the ways God cares for you and your son. Ask your son if there are specific things he would like to talk with God about. Pray together.

A Verse to Remember

You will keep in perfect peace all who trust
in you, whose thoughts are fixed on you!
Isaiah 26:3

"Uhh, Dad, We Have a Problem"

*D*ad's *acting kind of strange today,* Isaac thought. Old Abraham was packing a few things for a trip up the mountain, but something wasn't right. Isaac just couldn't put his finger on what it was. *It's not so odd that he wants to make a sacrifice to God. But he doesn't usually ask me to come along. Maybe he just wants me to learn how to do it,* Isaac thought.

God will provide, my son

Abraham led a donkey loaded with wood and a pot of fire up the mountain. Isaac ran ahead picking up stones and tossing them as far as he could. Suddenly Isaac knew what was wrong. Usually his dad took a lamb to be the sacrifice. "Father, we forgot . . ." Before he finished, Abraham put a finger to his lips; he knew what Isaac was going to say.

"God will provide, my son," Abraham said quietly.

They reached the top of the mountain and Abraham said, "Get some stones, son. We need to build an altar." Father and son worked quietly together. Isaac thought he had never seen his father so tense.

When the altar was built Abraham said, "Come here, son." Isaac's heart filled with fear! His own father tied up his hands and feet and laid him on the altar– HE WAS THE SACRIFICE!

"But Dad . . ." Isaac started to cry.

"Shhh. I love you with all my heart, Isaac, but I love God more. This is what he told me to do." Abraham was so upset that he could barely get the words out.

He raised his knife to sacrifice his own son when the voice of God's angel stopped him. "Wait. Don't hurt your son. You have shown that you love God more than anything and that is the way it should be."

Isaac didn't even realize he was holding his breath until he heard the angel's voice. Relief spread across his face as his father untied him. They hugged long and hard. Abraham caught a ram that God put in the bushes and together they sacrificed it to God. The sweet prayers of father and son, standing with arms around each other, were filled with praise to the God who would one day sacrifice his only Son.

Based on Genesis 22:1-14

Becoming a Man of God

A man of God loves God most of all

Isaac learned an important lesson at a young age: don't put anything—ANYTHING—ahead of God. Other things and people may be very important to you, but they should never be more important than God.

Who is important to you? Who do you love a whole bunch? Is that person sometimes more important to you than God?

Mom's Touch

Tell your son how important he is to you and how you thank God every day for him.

Share a time when something seemed more important to you than God—maybe it was a possession or maybe it was a position, such as a job or a part in a play. Maybe it was a person. Talk about how it became more important than God. How did you handle it?

Talk about what is important to your son. Encourage him to share what he really cares about. Talk about ways to keep God in first place.

A Verse to Remember

You are worthy, O Lord our God, to receive glory and honor and power. For you created everything, and it is for your pleasure that they exist and were created.

Revelation 4:11

Boys Will Be Boys

"MOM! Esau hit me!" Jacob screamed. Rebekah came running and found Jacob flat on the ground, Esau holding him down with a foot planted firmly on his chest. She sighed, wondering if her sons would ever outgrow this and be friends. They didn't.

When the boys grew up Jacob was a homebody. He helped Rebekah cook and take care of the house. Esau loved to be out hunting with his father. The brothers were like oil and water—they just didn't mix.

One afternoon Rebekah was cleaning when she heard her husband say, "Esau, I'm old and I'm sick. I know that I won't be around much longer. Since you are my oldest son, I want to give you the family blessing. This honor means you will lead the family after I die. Hunt some wild game, and cook my favorite meal for me. After I eat, I'll give you the blessing."

Rebekah threw down her broom. Years of Esau winning over Jacob and making fun of him welled up in her heart. She knew that she shouldn't favor one son over the other. But she did. She wanted to shout, "Jacob should have that blessing. It's time for him to win!" Instead, she went to Jacob and said, "Your father is ready to give the family blessing to your brother. But, I'm going to get it for you!"

"Oh, right. We're going to make Father think I'm Esau? Did you forget Esau has hairy skin, and mine is smooth?"

"Don't be snippy," Rebekah said tossing goatskins at him. "Put these on your arms so you feel like Esau."

When Jacob went to his father, Isaac was confused. "You sound like Jacob but you feel like Esau."

"I am Esau," Jacob lied. "Give me the blessing."

"May God bless you, may nations serve you, and may you rule over your brothers." It was done. Jacob had stolen Esau's blessing.

As soon as Esau found out what had happened he begged for a blessing, too. "Please, Father, you must have a blessing left for me!" But Isaac didn't. Esau angrily threw a chair against a wall. "I'll get even with Jacob!"

Jacob hid behind his mother, scared of Esau's anger. "It's OK, you just have to get away for awhile until he calms down," Rebekah said. Later, she watched as her favorite son left home. He had the blessing, but she wondered, *Will I ever see him again?*

Based on Genesis 27:1–28:6

Becoming a Man of God
A man of God learns from his mistakes

Whew! This mom and son made a big mistake, didn't they? Deep down inside, Jacob and Rebekah knew that it was wrong to steal the family blessing. They made a bad choice—we all do that sometimes. But, if they learned a lesson, then it wasn't a wasted experience.

Have you ever been jealous of someone who seems to always have better toys or get better grades or do things that are more fun than anyone else? Have you wanted to get something that you didn't really deserve? Did any of your friends or family get angry with you? What happened?

Mom's Touch

Has your son ever heard you admit that you have made a mistake? Has he heard you apologize to God and to the people who were hurt by your mistake?

Share an experience you had when you made a bad choice or a mistake. What happened? How did you settle the problem?

It's important for your son to realize that everyone makes mistakes so that he isn't too hard on himself when he does. Thank God for his forgiveness and his love.

A Verse to Remember

Though they stumble, they will not fall,
for the LORD holds them by the hand.

Psalm 37:24

Red Sea PANIC

The minute someone saw the Egyptian army chasing after them the people were in Moses' face, and his sister, Miriam, and his wife, Zipporah, watched it all.

"What's going to happen to us? Did you bring us out here to die? We should have stayed in Egypt!" Everywhere Moses looked he saw panicked eyes wide with fear.

Moses understood that the people were confused. God did ten awesome miracles to get them out of Egypt.

I know what happened, Moses thought. *Pharaoh must have realized that without us there was no one to make bricks and do the other slave work. So, Pharaoh and his whole army have come to bring us back. What a mess; the army is coming at us and we're trapped with our backs against the Red Sea!*

Moses pushed through the crowd of shouting people and climbed onto a big rock where he could be alone. He knelt down and poured out his heart to God. "Are my people going to die here? Are we going to be dragged back to slavery? Dear God, what is going on?"

Of course, God had a plan. He didn't bring his people to the desert just to leave them alone and let bad things happen. God told Moses exactly what to do.

"Be quiet!" Moses called to the frightened Hebrews. "Watch what God will do to save you!" He lifted his hand over the sea. Immediately the wind began to blow—harder and harder it blew. Mommas held on to babies and daddies held on to mommas. The wind blew so hard that the waters blew apart—two big walls of water stood high. It kept blowing until the ground between the walls was completely dry. "Go on through!" Moses cried. The scared people held back, until one man bravely stepped out, then all the people followed.

It took a long time for all the people to cross, even though they hurried as fast as they could—parents carrying children and young people helping old people.

The Egyptian army raced into the sea, sure that they could catch the Hebrews. But when Moses raised his hand over the sea again, the walls of water crashed down, flooding over the soldiers and chariots. Every Egyptian soldier died in the Red Sea that day, but God kept every Hebrew safe!

Based on Exodus 14

Becoming a Man of God
A man of God works for God

Way back at the burning bush when God first asked Moses to lead his people to freedom, Moses was scared. He didn't think he could do it. But now, God told him to raise his hand over the sea and Moses did it! He was willing to do whatever God told him to do.

Someday God may ask you to do something that you think is too hard. Remember that he won't ask you to do a job without promising to help you do it!

When have you had to do something that was hard or scary? Why was it scary? Were you able to do it?

Mom's Touch

Share a time when you had to do something that was very difficult for you. Why were you afraid? How did you get through it? How did you feel afterward?

Talk about the way that exercising the muscles in your body makes them stronger. It's the same way with our "spiritual muscles." Trusting God to help us do hard things and seeing how he helps makes our faith grow stronger.

A Verse to Remember

I can do everything with the help of Christ
who gives me the strength I need.

Philippians 4:13

Thank God for Second Chances!

"EEEIIIIYOOOOO!" Samson jerked the angry, roaring lion high up in the air and tossed it out of his way. Then he flipped his long black hair over his shoulder and went on his way. NO ONE ... not even a full-grown madder-than-anything lion messed with Samson. He was the strongest man in the world! No one could match his strength ... but he did have one weakness. Samson loved pretty girls. He liked to tease them, and he liked it when they teased back. This weakness was going to get him in big trouble!

Samson fell head-over-heels for a pretty Philistine girl named Delilah. The problem was that the Philistines hated Samson. (Once he had killed a bunch of Philistines, just using a donkey's jawbone, and the rest of them wanted to get even!) The sneaky Philistines came up with a plan. "Find out where Samson's strength comes from and we'll pay you big money!" they told Delilah. Right away money-hungry Delilah started whining and nagging Samson to tell her the secret of his strength.

Samson teased her, giving goofy answers—"New ropes will hold me" or "Tie me up with seven bowstrings and I'll be as weak as anyone." Each time Delilah did what he said and called the Philistines, but each time Samson flexed his muscles and escaped.

"You don't love me," Delilah pouted. "If you did you'd tell me the truth."

Samson couldn't stand to have her mad at him. "My strength comes from my long hair. It's never been cut because I was dedicated to God as a baby. If my hair were cut, my strength would be gone."

Aha! Now Delilah had him! She waited for Samson to fall asleep, then she called, "Come in, my Philistine friends, and bring your money. Cut his hair off and Samson is yours!" Strands of long, beautiful hair fell to the floor. Samson woke up while they were tying his arms and he tried to flex his muscles . . . but nothing happened. Laughing at him, the Philistines poked his eyes out and dragged him off to prison. Delilah stretched out on her bed and counted her money.

A while later the Philistines paraded Samson around at a big party. The people laughed and made fun of him. (No one noticed that his hair had grown back.)

"O God, help me one last time to beat the Philistines," Samson prayed. Then he put each hand on one of the giant pillars that held up the building and pushed with all his might. Almost in slow motion the pillars cracked and broke in half. The building crashed down, killing Samson and all the Philistines—more than he had killed in his whole life.

Based on Judges 16

Becoming a Man of God

A man of God doesn't let anything come between him and God

Samson blew it! As a young child he was dedicated to serve God. He didn't always behave in a way that showed God was important to him . . . especially in this story. His weakness for pretty girls came between him and God and ended up being his downfall. Thankfully, Samson realized his sin later, repented, and served God once again.

Is there anything or anyone that you really, really like and that could become more important to you than God? What is it? How do you make sure that you keep God in the most important place in your life?

Mom's Touch

Have you ever struggled with something or someone becoming more important to you than God? Tell your son about it and how it affected your relationship with God. How did you get things back on the right track? Is that thing or person still important to you?

Tell your son that it's OK to care about people or things, but he should never let something become so important that it pulls him away from God.

Pray with your son that you will both be able to keep God in the center of your lives, no matter what.

A Verse to Remember

Do not worship any other gods besides me.

Exodus 20:3

No Fear!

"**I**'m not scared!" David said firmly. "I mean it. I'm not scared of that big, ugly giant!" He stood with his feet spread apart and his hands on his hips. "How can all of King Saul's soldiers just let that big creep keep on makin' fun of them . . . and of God?"

That's exactly what the soldiers had been doing. Twice a day for forty days Goliath shouted, "Hey you Israelite chickens, send someone out to fight me. Come on. Winner takes all!" No one volunteered.

Every time David heard Goliath's shouts he got mad. "How can all these big, brave soldiers be scared of him, when I'm not . . . I'm just a kid!"

Suddenly David felt a hand grab his shoulder and squeeze it hard. "What are you doing here, you little show-off?" It was David's older brother and he was MAD! "Just go home; you don't belong here."

"I'll go—but not home!" David answered. He marched into King Saul's tent and announced, "I'll fight the giant!"

King Saul was excited to finally have a volunteer . . . until he looked at the skinny little boy. "What chance would you have against a nine-foot-tall giant?" But, he had to admit that the kid looked determined. "Well, OK, but at least wear my armor," he said.

David put it on, but the armor was so heavy that he couldn't take a step or lift his arms. "Get me outta this tin can!" he cried. "I gotta do this my way!"

As David went down the hill, he picked up some rocks and dropped one into his slingshot.

King Saul's soldiers ran to the top of the hill and watched the brave young man. "He's crazy!" "Nah, he's just stupid!" They didn't know WHAT to think.

When Goliath saw the kid with the slingshot and shepherd's staff, he was M-A-D! He glared at David and flexed his muscles and pounded his spear into the ground. David didn't even flinch!

As he got closer to Goliath, David swung his slingshot around and around over his head. It seemed to hypnotize the giant. Finally, David let go and the rock flew out of the sling and shot through the air. It landed right on Goliath's forehead. THUD! The nine-foot-tall giant looked totally shocked as he fell to the ground.

The Philistine soldiers saw their hero fall and they hightailed it down the hillside. The Israelite soldiers shouted and cheered, "He won! The little guy won!"

Based on 1 Samuel 18

Becoming a Man of God
A man of God trusts God's power

This scene must have looked pretty funny. All of King Saul's big brave soldiers stood around watching as a young boy went to fight the giant that they were all afraid of. Why were none of them able to fight Goliath? Because they didn't believe they had God's power to help them.

Have you ever had to do something that was really hard? What was it? Why was it scary? Did you ask God to help you? How do you know that he did help?

Mom's Touch

One way that your little guy will learn to trust in God's power is by seeing you trust God in your everyday life. He must learn to not only call on God in a crisis but to develop an everyday relationship with him.

Share a story with your son about a time when you knew without a doubt that God's power was helping you.

Ask your son what kinds of situations he finds difficult. Talk through what it is that frightens him. Pray together for God's help and for your son to KNOW when God is helping him. Remember to thank God for his help and constant care.

A Verse to Remember

The LORD is good. When trouble comes, he is a strong refuge.

Nahum 1:7

Loyal Buddies

"Jonathan, what have I done wrong? Why does your dad want to kill me?" David was scared. King Saul had chased him around the countryside and had even thrown sharp spears at him—and David didn't know what he had done.

"Oh come on, don't you think you're overreacting?" Jonathan asked. He leaned back and heaved a pebble high into the air. A few minutes later it landed with a soft splash in the nearby lake.

"Dad wouldn't hurt you. He's probably just playing around." Jonathan couldn't believe that his dad would really hurt David. "After all, he knows you're my best friend. Besides, Dad tells me everything he's planning to do. He hasn't said anything about being mad at you."

"Exactly; he knows we're good friends. He wouldn't tell you that he wants me dead because that would hurt you. But, I'm telling you that I am just one spear throw away from death!" David pounded his fist on his open palm to show how serious this matter was. "I have a plan," David said, "a way we can find out what he's thinking." David explained his idea to Jonathan.

The next day Jonathan sat down to eat a big dinner with his father. Everything was fine for awhile, then King Saul shouted, "Where's David?"

"He went to see his family," Jonathan said softly.

"Go get him so I can kill him!" King Saul shouted. He jumped up so fast that his chair flew back against the wall. "As long as he's alive, you'll never be king!"

Jonathan was sad. Now he knew that his father really did want to hurt David.

Jonathan went out to the field where David was hiding and shot three arrows. Then he sent a servant to get the arrows, "That one arrow is still ahead of you!" he shouted to the boy. That was the sign that meant King Saul wanted to kill David. When the boy left, David came out and the two friends hugged. Tears rolled down their faces because they knew that David had to leave and they might never see each other again.

Based on 1 Samuel 20

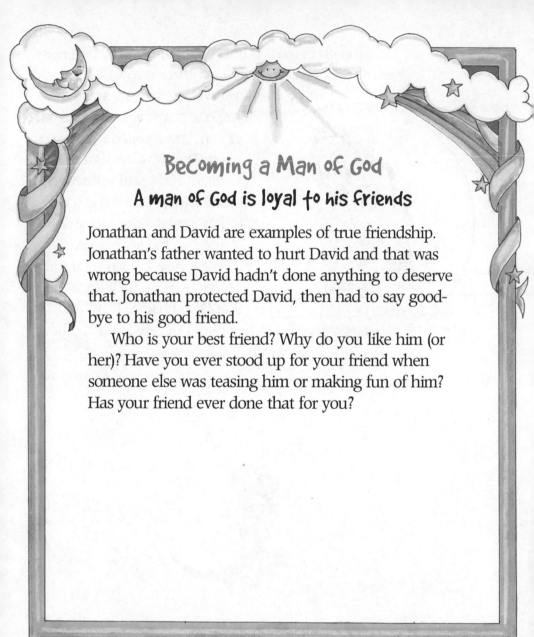

Becoming a Man of God

A man of God is loyal to his friends

Jonathan and David are examples of true friendship. Jonathan's father wanted to hurt David and that was wrong because David hadn't done anything to deserve that. Jonathan protected David, then had to say good-bye to his good friend.

Who is your best friend? Why do you like him (or her)? Have you ever stood up for your friend when someone else was teasing him or making fun of him? Has your friend ever done that for you?

Mom's Touch

Good friends make life a lot more fun. Happy times are happier when we share them with a friend, and sad times are easier, too.

Share a story with your son about a good friend you had while growing up. Share some of your experiences, especially if one of them shows you or your friend being loyal to one another.

Talk with your son about ways he can show loyalty to a friend. Talk about how a friend will feel if your son stands up for him when others are picking on him. Thank God for the special gift of good friends.

A Verse to Remember

A friend is always loyal, and a brother
is born to help in time of need.

Proverbs 17:17

The Real God—

"**M**ake up your minds!" Elijah shouted to the people. He was tired of them claiming to serve God one day, then some fake god the next day. "If God is God, then serve him and forget the others."

Elijah was the only one of God's prophets left, but the fake god, Baal, had 450 prophets. *Maybe it's time to force the issue*, Elijah thought. "I challenge you prophets of Baal to a contest. Meet me on Mt. Carmel and we'll see whose god is the real God!"

The prophets of Baal built an altar and put a bull on it. Then they danced around and called to Baal, "Send fire down and burn up our offering. Come on, Baal . . . yoohoo, Baal!" Elijah leaned against a tree watching this silliness.

Finally, he said, "Maybe Baal is sleeping, or in the bathroom. Maybe he's away on a trip." This just made them shout louder!

After listening to them scream all day Elijah finally said, "Enough already. It's my turn."

He built an altar and put a bull on it. Then Elijah did something strange. He dug a trench around the altar and poured four big jars of water over the whole thing . . . then he did it again . . . and again. Water overflowed the trench; the wood and the bull were soaked!

Elijah stepped back and said, "OK, God, show these people that you are the true God."

"Ahh! Watch it! Ow, it's hot!" People scrambled out of the way as tongues of fire shot down from heaven and burned up the bull, the altar, and even the water.

"My hair is burned."

"Yuck, that burned meat smells awful!"

The prophets of Baal stared at the smoky remains of the altar. Suddenly one of them shouted, "Let's get outta here!" and they dashed down the mountain. "Grab them!" Elijah shouted. He wasn't going to let them get away with insulting God.

Meanwhile, the crowd of people who had come up to see the contest fell to their knees and bent their faces all the way to the ground. "The Lord is God! The Lord is God!" they shouted.

Based on 1 Kings 18:19-40

Becoming a Man of God
A man of God takes a stand

Wow! One man takes a stand against 450 men. Elijah strongly believed in God. He was so sure that God was the real God that he could even make fun of the prophets of Baal when they tried to get Baal to answer them. Those guys could have gotten mad and tried to kill Elijah. But, he wasn't afraid.

Have you ever felt like you should take a stand for God when others were making fun of him? Have you ever heard kids making fun of someone who goes to church or some activity your church is planning? Did you try to stop them? It's not easy to stand up against a crowd, is it?

Mom's Touch

Share a story about some time when you were bothered by people making fun of something or someone. Did you take a stand or not? If not, did you later wish that you had? If you did, how did you feel later?

Discuss ways that your son can take a stand for God. He might be able to invite someone to church, or explain to someone why church is important to him. He might be able to explain why he feels some language or activity is wrong because it doesn't honor God. Encourage him to always speak in love and remind him that anytime he takes a stand God is right there to help him.

A Verse to Remember

Those who wait on the LORD
will find new strength.
They will fly high on wings like eagles.
They will run and not grow weary.
They will walk and not faint.

Isaiah 40:31

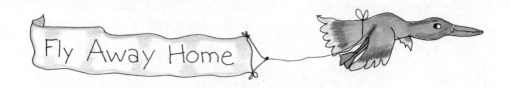

Fly Away Home

"I have so much to learn. I want to be with you every minute."
Elisha grabbed Elijah's arm. "I know God wants you to go
somewhere. But I want to come with you. Please, don't make me
stay behind."

Elisha had a feeling that Elijah wasn't going to be around much
longer, and he wanted to learn as much as he could from the great
prophet of God.

For the next few weeks Elisha followed Elijah
everywhere. He stuck closer than glue! Every
time they went to a new town someone
would say, "Did you know that God
is going to take your master away
soon?"

"Be quiet. Of course I know,"
Elisha always answered. He barely
even let himself sleep at night
because he wanted to soak up
everything Elijah knew and learn from
his close walk with God.

One afternoon Elijah and Elisha stopped near the Jordan
River. Elisha watched as Elijah carefully folded up his
robe. Then Elijah slapped his robe on the waters of the
Jordan River. "Wow! The waters are parting!" Elisha was
so surprised that he stumbled backwards and fell to the
ground. Elijah helped him to his feet, and they crossed the
Jordan River on dry ground. Elisha wasn't sure what this all
meant.

"What can I do for you before I leave?" Elijah asked.

"I want to be God's prophet like you are," Elisha answered.

"That's a tough request. But, if you see me when I'm taken away then you've got it." As Elijah finished speaking a chariot made of fire came between the two men. It was so bright that Elisha had to peek through squinted eyes to see. He was so frightened that he couldn't catch his breath, and his heart pounded so loud he was sure everyone could hear it. "Elijah is in the chariot and it's flying away!"

Elisha was so frightened that he couldn't even speak as the chariot disappeared. He stood looking at the sky for awhile, then picked up Elijah's robe from the ground. He folded it and hit the waters of the Jordan River with it. They divided, just as they had when Elijah hit them. Then Elisha walked across the river on dry ground and went right past a group of prophets from Jericho who had seen everything that happened. As he passed them, they shouted, "Elisha has taken Elijah's place!"

Based on 2 Kings 2

Becoming a Man of God
A man of God learns from older Christians

Elijah had served God for a long time, and Elisha knew that he could learn a lot from him. So he stayed very close to Elijah and watched everything he did. What a great way to learn! When Elijah left, Elisha knew just what to do, and he showed that by picking up the robe and smacking the waters of the Jordan River.

Who is an older person whom you admire a lot? Why? Do you think you could learn things from this person? What kinds of things could you learn?

Mom's Touch

This is a great opportunity to reinforce respect for those who are a little older and have lived a little more life. Share with your son about someone who has mentored you. This doesn't have to be a spiritual mentor, perhaps someone who taught you sports or guided you in developing parenting skills. Talk about what you learned.

Help your son think of older Christians who could help him grow in his Christian walk. What about Christians who could teach him other things like mechanics, fishing, baseball?

A Verse to Remember

And so my children, listen to me, for happy are all who follow my ways. Listen to my counsel and be wise. Don't ignore it.

Proverbs 8:32-33

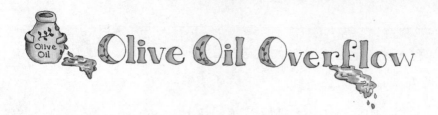

Olive Oil Overflow

"Momma, what is he talking about?" the little boy asked from behind his mother's skirt.

"Are we going to have to go live with that mean man, Momma?" her other son whispered.

Wasn't it enough that the boys' father had just died? Now this fellow shows up saying that her husband owed him lots of money—and if she doesn't pay up, he will take her sons to be his slaves.

"I'm not giving you up, boys," she said. "At least not without a fight." The frightened widow hurried to see Elisha. She knew that if anyone could help her, it would be a prophet of God.

She spilled her story to Elisha and he immediately asked, "What can I do to help you?"

"I don't know," the woman said. "I don't have any money so I can't pay the man what my husband owed. But, all I have left is my sons. Please don't let him take them!"

"Tell me what you have in your house," Elisha said.

"I'm telling you that I have nothing—except one jar of olive oil," she said sadly.

Elisha smiled. "OK, send your sons around to all your neighbors' houses. Have them borrow all the empty jars and bowls they can find."

The woman didn't even ask him why. She sent her sons out to the neighbors right away. When they returned, Elisha told her to take her one little jar of olive oil and pour it into one of the empty jars.

She did what he said. "This one is full. Bring another jar," she called to her son. Jar after jar after jar was filled to the brim from the woman's one little jar of oil. Her sons cheered the awesome miracle!

"Now," Elisha said, "sell all that oil and pay the man what you owe him. There will be enough money left over for you and your sons to buy food."

Based on 2 Kings 4:1-7

Becoming a Man of God
A man of God goes to God for help

The poor woman in this story was at the end of her rope. Her husband had died. She had no money. She had nothing left but her two precious sons, and now this man was threatening to take them away. But, this woman loved God. She knew that the best thing to do was ask God's prophet for help.

Any problem, any trouble that you might have is best handled by talking to God about it. The great thing to remember is that nothing happens to you without God knowing about it.

When have you had a problem that you didn't know how to solve? Did you talk to God about it? Sometimes a problem seems so bad that it's hard to know how to talk to God about it. That's when it's a good idea to talk to a grown-up like your mom, a Sunday school teacher, or minister. They can help you pray and tell God about it.

Mom's Touch

Tell your son about a difficult situation you have faced—either as a child or an adult. Tell him why it was hard or painful. Tell him how you prayed about it and how God helped you handle the situation.

Tell your son about a time when you just didn't know what to do about a problem. Tell him how you handled that—did you talk with a friend or pastor and discuss how to pray about it or what to do?

Remind your son that God sometimes helps us by showing us what to do, as he did the widow in this story. Sometimes having a great idea is the way God helps us solve a problem.

Ask your son if there is anything he would like you to pray about right now.

A Verse to Remember

If you need wisdom—
if you want to know what God wants
you to do—ask him and he will gladly tell you.

James 1:5

"We built this room for you to use when you come to town," the nice lady said to Elisha. He sat on the bed and bounced up and down—it was comfortable! He put some of his things on the table. It would be nice to have a place where he could keep stuff and come to rest sometimes. The lady and her husband were extra kind to Elisha. He was very thankful for them.

117

Later Elisha asked his servant, Gehazi, "What can I do to repay this kind woman? Is there anything she needs?"

"Hmmmm, the only thing I can think of is that she doesn't have a son and her husband is getting very old."

So, Elisha promised the woman that she would soon have a son.

"Oh, don't tease me!" the woman said. She couldn't believe it. But sure enough, about a year later, she had a bouncing baby boy. She was so happy!

The woman loved playing with her son, baking cookies for him, and watching him grow. The little boy loved his mom and adored his dad, following him around and copying everything he did.

One day the little guy was out in the field with his dad when he fell to the ground crying, "My head hurts; owww, my head." A servant carried him to his mom. She did everything she could think of . . . but her precious little boy died.

The heartbroken mother lay her son's body on Elisha's bed, brushed his hair back from his eyes, and sat with him for a long time. After a while, she knew what she had to do. Hurrying to Elisha she said, "Remember when I asked you not to tease me about having a son? Well, I had my son for just a little while; now he's dead." She cried and cried, holding on to Elisha's feet.

Elisha wanted to send his servant home with the woman to check on the boy. But she cried, "NO! I'm not leaving here without you!"

Finally, Elisha went with her to the boy. He prayed first, then did a strange thing: he stretched out on top of the boy—his face over the boy's face, his hands over the boy's hands. He stayed very still until he felt the boy's body getting warm. Suddenly the boy sneezed. "Achoo, achoo!" Seven sneezes and the boy was alive again! "Thank you!" the happy mother cried. The little boy was not quite sure what had just happened to him but he was very happy. The mother, the son, and Elisha praised God together.

Based on 2 Kings 4:8-37

Becoming a Man of God
A man of God helps others

Elisha was a busy man. He was a prophet of God so he had a lot of jobs to do and a lot of people to serve. But, Elisha knew this kind woman had a serious problem. Even though he may have been able to help her by just speaking a word or sending his servant, he went home with her because it was important to her to know that he cared that much.

Do you like to help other people? What kinds of things do you do that are helpful?

Mom's Touch

Do you have an example of a time when someone helped you? What did that person do? What did it mean to you? Did it make you feel as if that person truly cared about you?

Think with your son of ways that both of you can help others. Are there things that the two of you enjoy doing together? How can you show people that you care about them?

A Verse to Remember

This is the message we have heard from the beginning: We should love one another.

1 John 3:11

Veggie Power

"What makes King Nebuchadnezzar think we'd want to live in the palace? They're acting like it's such an honor!" Daniel and his three friends whispered to one another.

"Yeah, a whole year of training and special treatment . . . but we're still prisoners—just prisoners in a palace!" Daniel and his friends were Jewish boys captured by the Babylonians. Because they were young, healthy, and good-looking they were put in a special training program to become palace workers.

"You will be taught to speak our language. You will be taught the proper way to behave in the palace, and, best of all," the prison guard announced to the group of handsome young men, "you won't have to eat prison food. You will be served the king's best food and wine!"

"Yahoo! Filet mignon! Lobster! Duck L'orange!" The other boys danced around and cheered. But Daniel, Shadrach, Meshach, and Abednego weren't so happy.

"That food is offered to idols before it's served to us," Daniel whispered to his friends. "We can't eat it because it would not be honoring to God." The four friends huddled together and came up with a plan.

"Sir," Daniel addressed the guard very respectfully, "my friends and I wish to eat vegetables and water instead of the king's food."

"No way! If you aren't as strong as the other boys the king will have my neck!" the man shouted.

"Well, how about a test?" Daniel begged. "Give us vegetables and water for ten days; if we don't look as good as everyone else after ten days, we'll eat the king's food." The guard agreed, but he wasn't too sure about this plan.

"Yuck! Why are you eating green stuff when you could have steak and potatoes?" the other boys asked. They made fun of Daniel and his friends.

Veggie Power!!

But a strange thing happened. After ten days, Daniel and his friends were stronger and healthier than all the other boys!

"It's veggies and water for you guys from now on!" the guard laughed. God blessed Daniel, Shadrach, Meshach, and Abednego because they honored him. At the end of the training the king was more impressed with these four boys than any of the others.

Based on Daniel 1

Veggie Power!

Becoming a Man of God
A man of God refuses to compromise

Daniel and his friends were prisoners. They didn't have any rights at all. It was very brave of Daniel to ask for special permission to eat different food than the other prisoners. Their witness for God was very important to them and they weren't willing to compromise. That means they wouldn't take even one step away from what they believed was the right thing to do. These bright boys came up with a plan to keep from compromising. That was a great idea!

What are some things you know for sure are right? Would anyone be able to get you to change your mind?

Mom's Touch

Wow, Mom, this can be a lesson for adults, too, can't it? So many times at school, at work, or in the neighborhood, subtle little things tempt us to compromise our stand for Christ. Share an example of a time you were tempted to compromise, through doing something you weren't comfortable with, or a time when you didn't speak up for God, but knew that you should have. How did you feel—either because you did compromise or you didn't?

What are some ways your son may be tempted to compromise? Can you work together on a plan to solve the problem?

A Verse to Remember

You must love the Lord your God
with all your heart, all your soul,
and all your mind.
Matthew 22:37

Out of the Frying Pan and into the Fire

King Nebuchadnezzar thought he was pretty important and he wanted everyone to know it! "This giant ninety-foot-tall statue of me is so handsome. I want to be sure everyone notices it." So, the bragging king ordered that anytime his people heard music play, they should bow down and worship his big, golden statue!

"No way am I worshiping this statue," Shadrach declared. Meshach and Abednego agreed. The three friends loved God, and they knew it would be wrong to even pretend to worship anyone or anything besides him.

"Hey!" One of the king's guards poked Shadrach with his spear. "The king said to bow down and worship the statue. Are you three gonna hit the ground or what?"

"No, we're not," Shadrach said calmly.

"These guys refuse to bow to your statue!" the guard shouted, dragging the boys to the king.

"Is this true?" the king's voice boomed.

Shadrach took a deep breath and stood up tall. "Yes, Sir, we serve God and we will worship only him."

"GUARDS! Heat the furnace up hotter than ever. We're gonna make some Jewish french fries!" the king shouted. He was too angry to listen when Shadrach, Meshach, and Abednego said, "We trust our God to take care of us."

"So long, you stubborn fools!" A guard pushed the three boys into the blazing hot furnace. The fire was so hot that the guard burned to death! But, Shadrach looked over at his friends and they were doing fine. "It's hot alright, but we're not burning up. What's going on? This is strange!"

"Hey, how many guys did you throw in there?" the boys heard the king shouting at his guards.

"Three, your highness."

"Well then, who is that fourth guy in there? He kind of looks like an angel! GET THEM OUT HERE!" King Nebuchadnezzar roared.

Shadrach, Meshach, and Abednego weren't burned at all—they didn't even smell like smoke! "I told you our God would take care of us." Shadrach smiled.

"Yeah, I see what you mean," the king had to admit. "Your God is definitely awesome!"

Based on Daniel 3

"Awesome"

Becoming a Man of God

A man of God believes in God's protection

The boys in this story believed that God could protect them, even in a blazing furnace. It's easy to trust in God's protection when everything is going fine, but a scary situation like this is where the rubber meets the road.

Hopefully you haven't been in any scary or dangerous situations like these three boys. But someday you may be. The foundation of trust in God is like a tower that has a new layer added every day. What are the ways you see God's care and protection every single day?

Mom's Touch

The boys in this story took a stand for God and trusted him to do what was best—either protect them or bring them home to be with him. Either choice was fine with them. In today's world our children may be asked to take a stand for God and in some cases that stand may put them in danger. Help your son be ready by teaching him about God's care. Share a story of God's protection in your life, whether supernatural or as normal as being in a car going out of control.

Help your son think of ways God shows him protection every single day. Thank God for his care.

A Verse to Remember

The LORD says, "I will rescue those who love me. I will protect those who trust in my name."

Psalm 91:14

Here Kitty, Kitty

"**W**e have to get rid of Daniel! Did you hear that King Darius wants to make him our boss!"

"Yeah, but why should that Jew be so important here in Babylon? He's just a slave."

The jealous men looked and looked for ways to get Daniel in trouble with the king. But they couldn't find anything–Daniel was squeaky clean! Then one day, "Pssst, hey listen, I have a plan that will cook Daniel's goose. We're gonna trip him up with his own faith!"

The sneaky plan was to trick the king into signing a law that people couldn't pray to anyone except him.

Daniel heard about the new law, but he kept right on praying . . . to God! "I've talked to God my whole life. I respect King Darius, but I have to do what I know is right." He knelt in front of his bedroom window and poured out his heart to God. Little did Daniel know that his enemies were hiding behind a tree waiting for this exact thing to happen.

The bad guys tripped over each other in their hurry to tattle on Daniel. "Daniel prayed. We saw him! Throw him to the lions. It's the law; you can't change it...."

"I've been tricked," King Darius moaned. "I'm so sorry, Daniel, I have to obey the law," he said sadly.

"Don't worry. God will take care of me," Daniel said. He wasn't even a little bit afraid! The guards threw him into a pit full of hungry lions, then slid a big stone over the top. There was no way out!

It was a long night for the king. He paced around his room worrying about Daniel. "I know when the stone is moved tomorrow all that's left of Daniel will be picked clean bones."

King Darius would have been surprised to know that Daniel was doing fine. God protected him by sending angels to keep the lions' mouths locked tightly shut. They were as gentle as kittens all night long!

At the first peek of morning light King Darius rushed to the lions' den. "Daniel, did your God protect you?" he called.

"Yes, he did!" Daniel called back. "I haven't done anything wrong toward God or you, my king. So he kept the lions' mouths shut!"

"Hurray!" King Darius shouted. "Daniel's God is the real God. Everyone should worship him!"

Based on Daniel 6

Becoming a Man of God

A man of God knows God will do the right thing

Daniel knew that he hadn't done anything wrong. He obeyed and honored God just as he always did. There was no reason for him to be put to death. In his heart all he wanted to do was worship God and pray to him.

Daniel didn't hide his prayer because he knew that God knew his heart and that he could trust him no matter what.

Have you ever been accused of doing something wrong and had to trust a parent or a teacher to do the right thing? What happened?

Mom's Touch

Things can get a little scary when you must trust someone else to do the right thing on your behalf. Can you share an example of a time when you had to do that? How did it turn out? Can you also share an example of God's justice and fairness on your behalf?

Kids may often feel that they have no control over their lives because adults make all the decisions. Ask your little guy if he feels that way. Talk about ways for him to feel more involved in decisions. Talk about biblical examples of how God always does the right thing so that your son will know he can trust God completely.

A Verse to Remember

God is our refuge and strength, always
ready to help in times of trouble.

Psalm 46:1

The  Fish That Didn't Get Away!

"Nineveh? You want me to go to Nineveh? I don't like those people and if I tell them about you, they might repent of their sins and then–I know you–you would forgive them. No, I won't go!" Jonah stomped around the room and spilled out his anger. God didn't say another word to him. Jonah knew what he SHOULD do . . . but he also knew that he was NOT going to Nineveh!

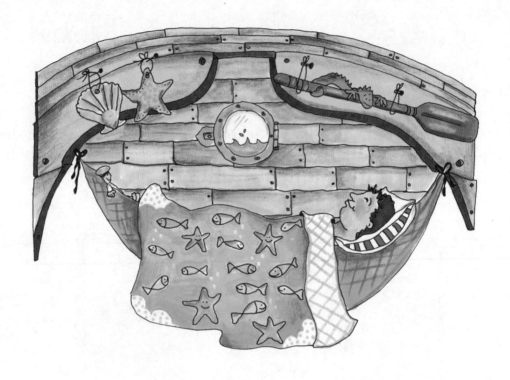

Throwing a few things in a bag Jonah ran for the first ship he saw. "Where you headed?" he called.

"Tarshish," the sailor shouted back. *Great! That's in the opposite direction of Nineveh,* Jonah thought. He went straight to the belly of the ship and lay down to sleep. *Hah! Not even God can find me here,* he thought as the rocking of the ship lulled him to sleep.

Meanwhile, the sailors had a problem ... "I've never seen a storm blow like this! It came out of nowhere. We're gonna sink. Do something! Throw boxes overboard! Lower the sails! Hurry!" Panicked sailors tossed whatever they could get their hands on— luggage, cargo, even food went into the boiling sea.

Jonah snorted and snored through the whole thing ... until a sailor shouted, "Get up! If you have a god, pray to him 'cause we've got big trouble!"

Right away Jonah knew what was happening. "Oh man, God found me after all."

"Look, this storm is all my fault—I was hiding from God. Toss me overboard and the storm will stop!" Jonah shouted over the roaring wind and splashing sea.

The sailors didn't want to hurt Jonah, but when they realized their choice was to toss Jonah or save their boat, Jonah went flying into the sea.

He had barely hit the water when a huge fish swallowed him right down. For three days and nights Jonah dodged sea junk in the great fish's belly. "Yuck, I'll never eat fish again!" he said.

Something else Jonah did was think about how he had disobeyed God. He felt bad. "I'm sorry, God. I should have obeyed you. If you still want me to go to Nineveh, I'll go." In a giant burp the big fish spit Jonah onto the beach. Yanking seaweed from his neck and minnows from his ears, Jonah ran for Nineveh.

Based on Jonah 1–4

Becoming a Man of God
A man of God obeys immediately

Jonah should have obeyed God the first time. Since he didn't, he got a free ride in the big fish's belly. But God gave him a second chance and by then Jonah had decided to do the right thing.

How many times has your mom asked you to do something and you have answered, "In a minute!" then you never do what she asked? That's sort of what Jonah did—only he never meant to obey.

When was a time that you didn't obey and were punished? What was the punishment? Did you learn a lesson from this experience?

Mom's Touch

Remember what it's like to be a child? There is always someone telling you what to do. Obeying is a constant challenge. Recall a time when you didn't obey your parents right away. What happened? How did you feel?

Remind your son of a time he did obey you immediately and tell him how proud you were of him. Reinforce obedience every chance you get.

Talk with him about what kinds of instructions he has trouble obeying right away and brainstorm ways you can make it easier.

A Verse to Remember

When you obey me, you remain in my love,
just as I obey my Father and remain in his love.

John 15:10

Read My Lips!

"You look like you saw a ghost," a friend said to Zechariah. "Not a ghost—an angel," Zechariah screamed . . . well, he wanted to scream, but when he opened his mouth nothing came out but air! God took away his voice because he didn't believe the angel's message.

Zechariah finished his work at the temple and hurried home to his wife, Elizabeth. He had something important to tell her—if he could make her understand.

152

"Are you crazy?" Elizabeth had never seen her husband like this. As a priest, Zechariah was normally quiet and kind of stuffy. But here he was jumping around, waving his arms and trying to speak, but no sound came out. "You have something to tell me, right? Just say it!" Elizabeth was frustrated . . . so was Zechariah. Finally, he grabbed her broom and scratched something in the dirt with the handle. He stepped aside so Elizabeth could read, "We're going to have a baby."

"Now I know you're crazy. You know how old I am. Do you seriously think a baby could grow in this shriveled old body?" Elizabeth grabbed her broom and started back to the house. But when she glanced back at Zechariah's face, she stopped. "You're serious, aren't you?" Suddenly her knees felt weak. She had to sit down. *A baby*, she thought. *After all these years I'm going to have a baby!*

The next few months were spent getting ready for the blessed event—Zechariah built a cradle, Elizabeth knitted booties. "Come quick!" she would call to Zechariah and he would run to put his hands on her growing tummy and feel their son kick. Sometimes he got frustrated that he couldn't tell his wife how excited he felt about the birth of their child—the special child who would grow up to tell the world that the Messiah was coming!

When their precious baby boy was born, all of Zechariah and Elizabeth's relatives came to help them celebrate. Everyone had an opinion of what the baby's name should be. In the middle of the shouting, Zechariah took a tablet and scratched HIS NAME IS JOHN and held it up for all to see. (That's what the angel had said to name him.) Immediately Zechariah's voice came back, and he and Elizabeth praised God together!

Based on Luke 1:5-25, 57-64

Becoming a Man of God
A man of God is sometimes quiet

Zechariah was alone in the temple doing his work as a priest, so it was probably quiet. When he didn't believe the angel's message and God took his voice away it was definitely quiet.

It's very hard to hear God speak, or anyone else for that matter, if you are always making noise.

Do people ever tell you to "Calm down" or "Use your inside voice"? Why do you think that happens? When someone is trying to explain something to you, do you listen quietly?

Mom's Touch

More than likely being quiet is not one of your little guy's strong points since most little boys like to make noise. Talk about what he might miss if he isn't sometimes quiet.

Share a story of a time when you didn't listen quietly and you missed some instructions or information. What happened?

If your son does listen quietly tell him how much you appreciate that. Then, go outside together and sit quietly. Listen to all the sounds around you.

Remind your son that God sometimes speaks in a whisper that we hear inside our hearts. If we're always noisy, we might miss what he's saying to us.

A Verse to Remember

Be silent and know that I am God.

Psalm 46:10

Night ✦ Flight

Sometimes Joseph nearly forgot that Jesus wasn't a boy like every other boy. He laughed, slept, burped, spit up, just like any other little one. But the truth slammed into Joseph's heart the day some wise men from another country showed up on fancy camels with colorful blankets on them. They brought fancy gifts to Jesus and worshiped him. Joseph noticed that Mary was taking everything in but not saying a word as she cradled Jesus in her arms. *I wonder what is ahead for this little guy*, he thought.

A few days after the wise men left, the angel visited Joseph's dream again. "Get your little family out of town! Quick! King Herod wants to kill Jesus!" Joseph felt his heart leap into his throat. His stomach hurt and a cold sweat broke out on his forehead. *God is trusting us to raise his son*, he thought. *I can't let Herod hurt him!*

"Mary, get up. Dress the baby. We have to leave town now," Joseph called. Mary got up and began to pack a few things before she woke the baby. "No! We don't have time to pack. We must hurry. Jesus' life is in danger!" That got Mary moving. In just a few moments she was on the donkey with Jesus sleeping in her arms. Joseph walked ahead of them, and the little family disappeared into the darkness outside of Bethlehem.

Joseph, Mary, and Jesus settled in Egypt. *I wonder how long we'll be here*, Mary wondered. It was hard to live in a foreign land where the people spoke a different language and their customs were different. The Egyptians didn't even worship God.

Finally, one night the angel came back to Joseph's dream. "King Herod is dead," the angel said. "It's safe to take Jesus home now."

Joseph and Mary were so happy to be able to go home. They quickly packed a few things for the trip. Instead of returning to Bethlehem, the little family went home to Nazareth. It was so good to see family and friends again! "Momma, Poppa, I've missed you so much. This is our son, Jesus!" Mary cried. Finally, Mary and Joseph could introduce Jesus to their family! It was good to be home.

Based on Matthew 2:1-23

Becoming a Man of God
A man of God protects

Joseph could have refused to run to Egypt. He could have said that he would stay in Bethlehem and fight for Jesus' safety. But Joseph was smart enough to know that he should follow any instructions an angel gave him because the most important thing was to protect Jesus from King Herod.

When has your mom or dad protected you? It's a nice feeling to know that someone is keeping you safe, isn't it?

Mom's Touch

When your children are small you spend a lot of time protecting them from the dangers they don't understand. Share a time when you remember protecting your son. Tell him how very much you love him and how glad you are that he is safe and healthy.

Ask your son if he understands that the rules you make for him are usually for his protection. Talk about ways your son can protect others–a younger sibling or a pet–ways he can show responsibility. Talk about some of God's rules and how they are for our protection. Thank him for his protection.

A Verse to Remember

The LORD keeps watch over you as you
come and go, both now and forever.

Psalm 121:8

A Child Shall Lead Them

"**I**'m so excited!" Jesus could barely sit down to dinner. "I love going to Jerusalem for the Passover Festival. Can I walk with my friends, huh, can I?"

"Hmm, I think you're old enough to walk with your friends this year." Mary smiled. "But sit down and eat dinner now. We still have lots to do before we leave tomorrow morning."
Jesus obeyed his mother, as he always did, but it was all he could do to sit still and finish dinner.

"Jesus, over here!"

Early the next morning Jesus was dressed and waiting at the door when his parents got up. Soon they were in the middle of the crowd walking to Jerusalem. "Jesus, over here!" someone called. He ran to join his friends and they laughed and played games as they walked. The Passover celebration was wonderful! Jesus and the other children were quiet and respectful as they and their parents thanked God for taking care of his people.

When the festival ended, the tired worshipers headed home. "Have you seen Jesus?" Mary asked.

"No, he's probably with his friends," Joseph answered.

A while later one of Jesus' friends came up. "Where's Jesus?" he asked.

"We thought he was with you," Mary answered.

"No, none of the guys have seen him all day." A stab of fear sank deep into Mary's heart as she shouted, "Jesus is lost!"

Mary grabbed Joseph's hand and they ran back to Jerusalem. They ran until their sides hurt and their breath came in short gasps so strong that they couldn't speak. "He's only twelve. What will happen to him in the big city? How could we lose him?" Mary's panicked heart cried.

For three long days Mary and Joseph searched the city, up and down the streets, every nook and cranny, everywhere they could think to look. Jesus was nowhere to be found!

They had nearly given up when they heard someone mention a boy who was teaching the temple teachers about God. Immediately, Mary and Joseph ran to the temple. It was Jesus! "Do you know what we've been through? We've looked everywhere for you," Mary cried.

Jesus calmly answered, "Didn't you know that I would be in my Father's house?" Then he went home with Mary and Joseph. They were so relieved that he was OK that they couldn't stop touching his arm or ruffling his hair.

Based on Luke 2:41-52

Becoming a Man of God
A man of God never gives up

Imagine the panic Mary and Joseph must have felt. God trusted them to take care of his son . . . and they lost him! Immediately Mary and Joseph began searching for Jesus. They looked for one day and they didn't find him, then they looked for another day but they didn't find him. But, Mary and Joseph didn't give up—they kept looking and looking until they found Jesus.

The best things in life take hard work to achieve. Have you ever worked really hard to learn something? Maybe you wanted to give up, but you didn't; you kept trying and trying until you learned it. Did you feel like celebrating when you finally learned what you had been working on?

Mom's Touch

Share a story with your son detailing your own perseverance. Tell him about something you had to work constantly to achieve or learn. Let him know how you struggled with it, maybe wanting to give up, but you kept on going.

Remember when you were a child? Big projects or long-term projects sometimes were overwhelming. It was hard to stick with something until it was finished. If you have seen your son stick with a project to completion, compliment him on that perseverance. Talk about areas where he might need to work on sticking with a project. Help him make a plan to do so.

A Verse to Remember

Hold on to the pattern of right teaching you have learned from me. And remember to live in the faith and love that you have in Christ Jesus.

2 Timothy 1:13

Go Fish!

"**W**ould you mind pushing the boat out from shore a bit?"
Who does this guy think he is? Peter wondered. *He climbs into my boat and sits down like he owns the world.* But, for some reason Peter didn't kick the guy out. In fact, he pushed the boat out just as the man had asked. He went on cleaning his nets while he listened to the man teach the crowd of people on shore. His voice echoed off the water like he was using a loud speaker.

When the man finished teaching, Peter expected him to get out of the boat and leave. But, instead the man said, "Go out there where the water is deeper and let your nets down. You'll catch lots of fish."

Yeah right, Peter thought, a sarcastic smile on his face. *I've been fishing this lake my whole life, and this guy is telling me where to catch fish?*

"Look, my partners and I worked hard all night and we didn't catch a single fish. We're tired— so—thanks anyway but we'll just go on home and get some sleep," Peter said. The man just quietly looked at Peter. For a few minutes Peter seemed to be fighting with himself about what to do. Finally, he took a deep breath and said, "OK. If you want us to try fishing over there, we'll fish over there."

"What's going on?" Peter screamed. He dropped his fishing net into the water and it instantly filled with so many fish that he couldn't pull it up. "Stop!" he called to his partners. "Don't pull anymore. The net is ripping! Someone help us! We've got so many fish we can't pull them in."

Peter looked over at the man who had a slight smile on his face. Suddenly Peter knew in his heart that this man was special . . . holy . . . the Son of God!

Peter dropped to his knees—he had never been in the presence of a holy man before. But, Jesus pulled him to his feet. "Don't be afraid," he said. "From now on you will fish for people!" Peter and his partners knew deep in their hearts that Jesus was special. They left their fishing boats right there on the shore and went with him.

Based on Luke 5:1-11

Becoming a Man of God
A man of God follows Jesus

Jesus has different jobs for each of us to do, because each of us is different. Peter was a fisherman before he met Jesus, so Jesus explained that Peter's work would now be to fish for men; in other words, Peter would tell other people about Jesus and his love. Peter was willing to leave his old life behind and follow Jesus.

Do you need to leave something in your "old life" behind to follow Jesus? Are you ever selfish or grumpy? How about disobedient? To be serious about following Jesus, you must leave those things behind and start a new way of living.

Mom's Touch

Jesus wants us to follow him and the goal of that following is to bring other people to him. Share with your son the story of who led you to Christ. That person was following Jesus. Tell your son how you share Christ with people. Maybe you teach Sunday school, sing in the choir, help a needy neighbor, volunteer in the food pantry, or make friends with people who don't know Christ.

Discuss ways your son can be a "Jesus follower" and tell people about Jesus, either by how he lives his life, or by inviting them to church.

A Verse to Remember

Come, be my disciples, and I will show
you how to fish for people!

Matthew 4:19

STORM WARNING

"**M**an, I'm tired. How does Jesus keep going?" Peter said.

"I don't know, I'm beat, too. But you know Jesus—as long as there are people who want to hear about God, he will keep teaching," John said through a big yawn.

The disciples were sprawled on the ground. Some slept, some chewed on blades of grass. They were listening to Jesus teach and he had been teaching for hours.

"Looks like he's finally wrapping it up," Peter said. "Let's get going."
But instead of going to the nearby town, Jesus said he wanted to
cross the lake. "I was hoping we could just go to town and get some
dinner," one disciple said.

"Shh," Peter whispered. "You know as well as I do that it's best
to do what Jesus says." Without another word the disciples climbed
into a boat and raised the sail. Jesus went to sleep in the back of the
boat.

About halfway across the lake the wind picked up and began bouncing the little boat all around.

"Lower the sail!"

"We're taking on water—start bailing!"

The waves tossed fish onto the deck and they flipped and flopped. "Oh wow! We're going down. We're all going to drown out here! WHERE'S JESUS?"

Someone ran to the back and poked Jesus on his shoulder. "Wake up! Don't you care that we're going to drown?"

Jesus stood up and looked out at the big waves. "Be quiet!" he shouted. Instantly the sea was calm again. The wind stopped, the rain stopped, and the waves were gentle.

"Whoa. What just happened here?"

"How did he do that?"

Jesus calmly looked around at his friends. "Where is your faith?" he asked. He sounded sad.

Jesus laid down again, but the disciples kept asking each other, "Who is he? How come the wind and waves do what he tells them to do?"

Based on Luke 8:22-25

Becoming a Man of God

A man of God believes Jesus can do anything

The disciples were scared even though Jesus, the Son of God, was with them on the boat. They were scared of the storm because they didn't understand that Jesus is more powerful than any storm—or anything else!

What kinds of things scare you? Why do they scare you? Do you talk to God about those things?

Mom's Touch

Tell your son of a time you were afraid. What frightened you? Was it a storm or an earthquake or maybe just the darkness of a quiet night? How did you get through your fear?

Ask your little guy what he's afraid of. Read the story of Jesus calming the storm again. Remind your son of God's awesome power and constant love. Pray together about the things that frighten you. Thank God that he will take care of you.

A Verse to Remember

The LORD is king!
Let the earth rejoice!
Psalm 97:1

Bread and Fish for Everyone!

"**M**om! Jesus is in town teaching about God! Can I go? Mom, please, can I go?" The little boy bounced up and down around his mother.

"Well, I guess so, but let me make a lunch for you."

"Oh, Mom, I don't need a lunch," the boy whined, edging toward the door.

"Oh, right. You're 'starving' every ten minutes, and you don't need a lunch. It will take me five minutes!"

Wow! There's thousands of people here! the boy thought as he picked his way through the crowd. He found a spot close to the front and sat down to listen. No one said a word for hours as Jesus talked about God's love. Pretty soon one of Jesus' helpers said, "It's late, Master. Send the people home for dinner."

If the boy were braver he would have shouted, "I don't want to go yet. Please, Jesus, keep teaching!" He almost cheered out loud when Jesus said, "No. You give them dinner."

"We don't have any food or any money to buy it," the man argued.

"Sir, you can have my lunch if you want." The little boy held up his small bundle.

Jesus' helper sneered at the little lunch. "That won't do any good with all these people!"

The little boy hung his head, feeling silly for thinking his little lunch could help.

A gentle hand slowly lifted the boy's chin. Jesus smiled as he took the little lunch and prayed, "Thank you, God, for this food."

Then he broke the bread and fish into pieces and the disciples passed it out to the people. They kept coming back and Jesus kept giving them more and more. *How did he do that?* the boy wondered, munching on his second helping.

Jesus' helpers walked through the crowd, picking up leftover food. "There must be five thousand people here! Everyone ate all they wanted and there are twelve baskets full of leftovers!"

The boy's skin prickled like someone was watching him. He looked around and saw Jesus smiling at him! "Wow! Just 'cause I shared my lunch I got to help with a miracle!"

Based on John 6:1-13

Becoming a Man of God

A man of God shares

When the little boy brought a lunch that day, he had no idea he was going to be able to help with a miracle. When he heard that Jesus needed food for the people, the little boy gave his whole lunch. He didn't take out some for himself or hold some back. He shared it all.

Do you have something that you don't like to share? Maybe it's a favorite toy or book. How do you feel when a friend doesn't share with you?

Mom's Touch

Mom, tell your son a sharing story—a time when someone shared something special with you and how you felt about that person after that. Tell about a time when you shared, or didn't share, and how you felt afterward.

Encourage your son to share generously. Point out a time when you noticed him sharing and tell him how proud you were of him.

A Verse to Remember

Do for others what you would
like them to do for you.

Matthew 7:12

Ghost Man Walking?

"**H**ey, do you see something out there on the water?"
"Yeah, it looks like some kind of sea monster."
"Nah, it's a . . . ghost!"
"Oh, come on. Get real."
"Well, then what do you think it is? There's something out there. Even in this storm I can see something." The disciples leaned out over the water and squinted their eyes, trying to make out what the thing was.

John shivered a little. "I wish Jesus was here. I always feel better when he's with us."

"Yeah, me too. And besides whatever is out there, this storm is getting pretty bad. I hope our boat doesn't take on much more water."

"Oh boy. That thing out there is getting closer! You'd think with this storm blowing so hard we'd be all the way across the lake by now." John pushed Peter in front of him and hid behind the big fisherman's back.

"It's a ghost! O God in heaven, protect us!" Even big brave Peter squeezed his eyes shut in fear.

"Hey, don't be afraid. It's me!" Peter opened one eye and saw what looked like Jesus walking on top of the stormy water.

"Jesus, if it's really you, let me walk to you on the water!" Peter was climbing out of the boat as he shouted.

"All right. Come on."

Peter almost ran across the top of the water until a big wave smacked him in the face. Suddenly he realized, "What am I doing?" At that very instant, it felt like the top of the water cracked and Peter quickly dropped into it. "Help! Help me!" He splashed and kicked and coughed.

Jesus pulled him up and as Peter coughed and gasped Jesus said, "You don't have much faith, do you? Why didn't you believe I could keep you safe?"

The other disciples helped Peter and Jesus climb into the boat. When they were safely inside, the wind suddenly stopped blowing. Stars glittered in the night sky, shining on the quiet sea.

Each of the tired men dropped to his knees in awe and worship. "This man really is the Son of God," one of them whispered.

Based on Matthew 14:22-33

Becoming a Man of God

A man of God keeps his eyes on Jesus

Peter jumped out of the boat and started walking on the water. He did fine as long as he kept his eyes on Jesus. But the minute he started looking around at the waves and the storm, he started sinking–he took his eyes off Jesus, the one who could keep him safe.

Some things, like hitting a baseball, can't be done unless you keep your eyes on what you're doing. If you take your eyes off the ball and swing the bat–you miss the ball. How good are you at keeping your eyes on what you're doing, no matter what else is going on?

Mom's Touch

Share with your son some activity you did as a child that required focus. Did you play a sport such as tennis, basketball, baseball, or did you play a musical instrument, or do needlepoint? All those activities require staying focused and keeping your eyes on what you're doing.

Talk with your son about how important it is to keep our eyes on Jesus. How do we keep our eyes on him? By reading God's Word and learning about him and by praying and listening for him to speak to us.

A Verse to Remember

Praise the LORD,
I tell myself, and never forget
the good things he does for me.

Psalm 103:2

Dad Always Liked You Best

"**I**'m sick and tired of this farm! I want more excitement! Bright lights and city life are for me!"

"Quit complaining and get busy. We have to get this fence mended today." The older brother was tired of his younger brother's whining and even more tired that he had to constantly nag him to get his work done.

"Well, you can stay on this farm 'til you rot, but I've got a plan and I'm going to be out of here quicker than you can say, 'Hand me a hammer!' "

That evening the young son had a talk with his father. "Dad, I need more excitement than I get watching wheat grow. How about if you give me my inheritance now? Then I can move to the big city and have some fun!"

His father sadly gave him the money and watched his young son leave home. The minute the boy hit the city, he started spending— fancy restaurants, big parties, gifts for his new friends. In no time at all the money was all gone.

"I left home to get away from farm stuff. Now the only job I can find is feeding pigs. What stinks is that they have food to eat and I don't! I hate to do it, but I'd better crawl back to Dad on my hands and knees and ask if he will let me be one of his hired hands. I don't deserve to be his son anymore. I've made some bad choices!"

When the boy got close to home, his father ran to meet him. "You're home! Hurrah! I've been waiting for you!" The boy tried to ask about being a hired worker. But, he couldn't get a word in edgewise.

"Cook a fancy meal. Put a purple robe and gold ring on the boy. My son is home and we're going to party all night!" The boy had never seen his dad so happy!

Meanwhile the older son worked away out in the fields. He heard music and laughter up at the house and came home to see what was going on. When he heard about the party he said, "I've been stuck here—doing my work and my brother's. I'm not going to a party for him! No one ever threw a party for me, even though I've been the good son all this time!"

The servant told the father about the older boy's feelings. The father went to see his son. "Don't you understand? I thought your brother was dead, but now here he is—alive and well. Best of all, he's home. I have to celebrate!"

Jesus told this story to show an example of how God forgives us for doing wrong things and welcomes us back to him.

Based on Luke 15:11-32

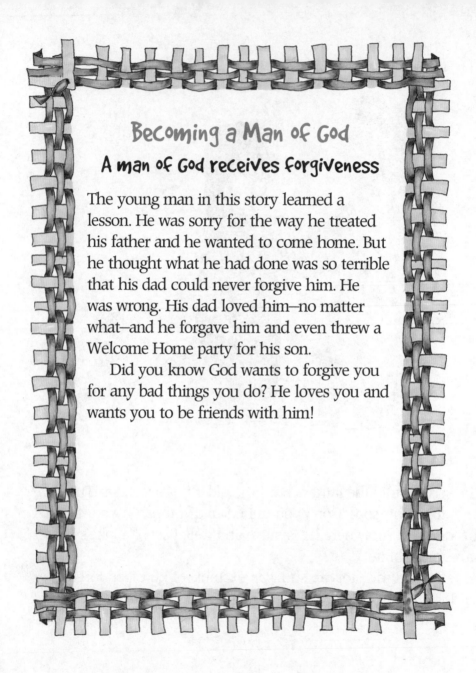

Becoming a Man of God

A man of God receives forgiveness

The young man in this story learned a lesson. He was sorry for the way he treated his father and he wanted to come home. But he thought what he had done was so terrible that his dad could never forgive him. He was wrong. His dad loved him—no matter what—and he forgave him and even threw a Welcome Home party for his son.

Did you know God wants to forgive you for any bad things you do? He loves you and wants you to be friends with him!

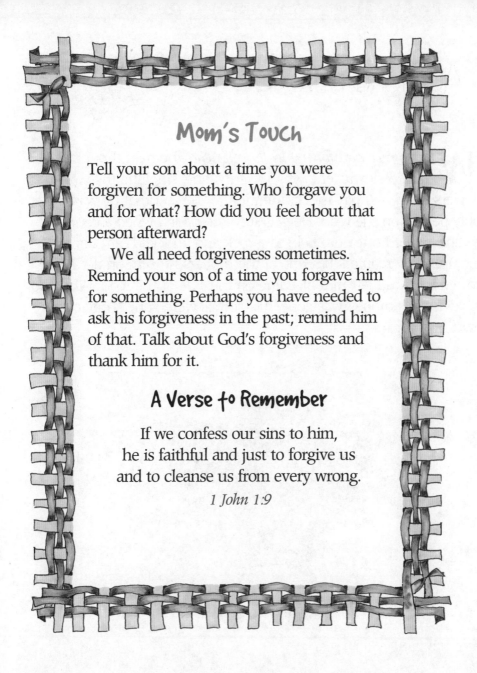

Mom's Touch

Tell your son about a time you were forgiven for something. Who forgave you and for what? How did you feel about that person afterward?

We all need forgiveness sometimes. Remind your son of a time you forgave him for something. Perhaps you have needed to ask his forgiveness in the past; remind him of that. Talk about God's forgiveness and thank him for it.

A Verse to Remember

If we confess our sins to him,
he is faithful and just to forgive us
and to cleanse us from every wrong.

1 John 1:9

A Friend in Need Is a Friend Indeed

What a nice day for my walk to Jericho, the man thought. He walked slowly, enjoying the sunshine, smelling the sweet flowers. He didn't pay much attention to the fact that he was the only person on the road. He was sorry he hadn't when a couple of creeps jumped out from behind a rock and knocked him down. "Let me up!" he screamed. But one of the robbers hit him on the head with a rock and left him bleeding on the side of the road. When he woke up, his money was gone, his clothes were gone. They even took his shoes!

They just left me on this deserted road to bleed to death. That's just what is going to happen, too, he thought. When he heard footsteps later, he struggled to lift his head. "Hurrah! A priest. If anyone will help me a priest will."

But to his surprise the priest looked at him with disgust. "Ugh! Why is this piece of garbage in the road!" Then he crossed the road and kept right on walking.

The sun beat down on the poor man. He had nearly given up hope when he once again heard footsteps. This time he didn't have the strength to lift his head, but squinting through half-opened eyes, he saw a temple worker coming toward him. The poor man lifted his hand and weakly called, "Help me. Please help me!" The temple worker came up to the man and poked him with his toe. *Hmm, this fellow has been beaten up pretty bad,* he thought, *but I'm busy. I've got work to do.* He stepped over the man and kept right on walking.

It was nearly dark before the man heard more footsteps. This time he didn't even open his eyes until he felt a gentle hand lift his head and slide a pillow under it. *A Samaritan. Samaritans hate us Jews. Why would you stop to help me? Do you think you're going to rob me? Sorry, buddy there's nothing left,* the hurt man thought, closing his eyes.

He must have gone to sleep because he woke up to find that he was lying in a soft bed in a nice inn. The Samaritan was cleaning his cuts and putting bandages on them. Then he saw the good Samaritan give the innkeeper gold pieces to take care of him. The man sighed and let himself relax. He knew he didn't have anything to worry about now.

Jesus told this story to make people think about who they should be helping.

Based on Luke 10:30-37

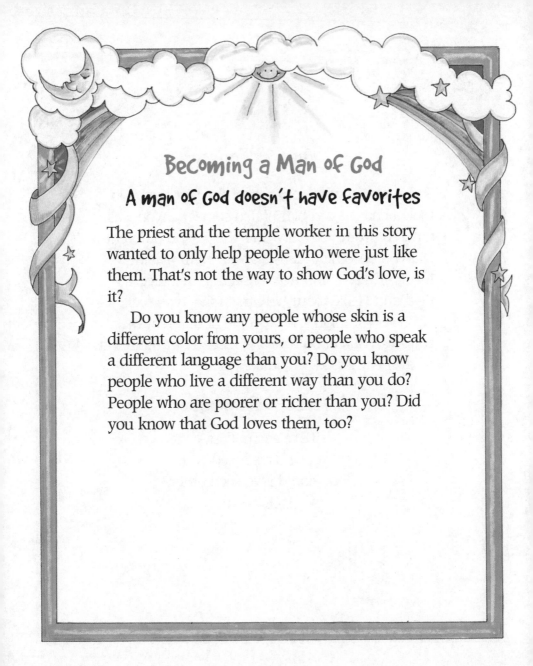

Becoming a Man of God

A man of God doesn't have favorites

The priest and the temple worker in this story wanted to only help people who were just like them. That's not the way to show God's love, is it?

Do you know any people whose skin is a different color from yours, or people who speak a different language than you? Do you know people who live a different way than you do? People who are poorer or richer than you? Did you know that God loves them, too?

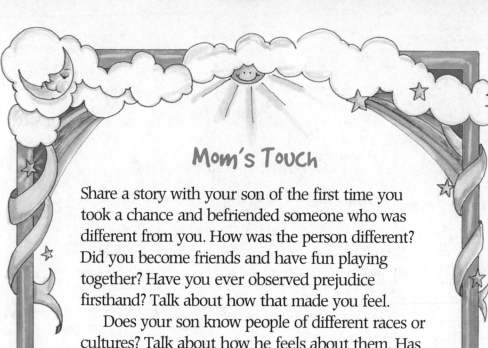

Mom's Touch

Share a story with your son of the first time you took a chance and befriended someone who was different from you. How was the person different? Did you become friends and have fun playing together? Have you ever observed prejudice firsthand? Talk about how that made you feel.

Does your son know people of different races or cultures? Talk about how he feels about them. Has he ever witnessed prejudice?

A Verse to Remember

Love each other.
Just as I have loved you,
you should love each other.

John 13:34

Through the Roof

E very day was exactly the same for the man. His legs didn't
work so he lay in bed all day . . . every day. He couldn't get his
own breakfast, go to work, or even pick up something he dropped.
The highlight of his day was when one of his good friends walked
through the door. *That's one thing I have to be thankful for*, the man
often thought. *I have wonderful, helpful friends.*

Four of the man's good friends often stopped by to talk. They laughed and remembered the old days when he went fishing with them, or played a game of catch.

One night the friends left the crippled man in bed and started home. "Wish there was something we could do to help him," one man said. That started everyone talking . . . soon the four friends came up with an incredible plan . . . that just might work!

The next day they were all back at their friend's house. One of them carried a cot that had a handle at each corner. "One, two, three," they shouted, and at the count of three they lifted their crippled friend onto the fancy cot.

"Where are we going?" the man asked. But his friends just told him to lean back and enjoy the ride. They carried him through town—he saw places he hadn't seen in years—to a little house crowded with people listening to Jesus of Nazareth teach about God's love.

"Coming through!" the men shouted, trying to part the crowd and get their friend to Jesus. But, instead of moving aside, the crowd moved closer together. Everyone wanted to see Jesus—and they weren't letting anyone cut to the front of the line!

Well, that's that, thought the crippled man. *At least my friends tried. I know Jesus could heal me if he wanted to, but not if they can't get me to him.* However, the four friends didn't give up so easily; they huddled together and came up with Plan "B."

The men grabbed the cot and ran to the rooftop. "What are you doing?" the crippled man cried, holding on for dear life. No one answered. They dug at the grass and tiles on the roof, keeping at it until there was a hole big enough to lower his cot into the room—right in front of Jesus.

The gentle teacher looked up at the four friends peering through the hole in the roof. When he saw their faith in him, he said to the crippled man, "Get up and walk." He did! Dust and dirt showered everyone in the room as four happy men danced on the roof.

Based on Mark 2:3-12

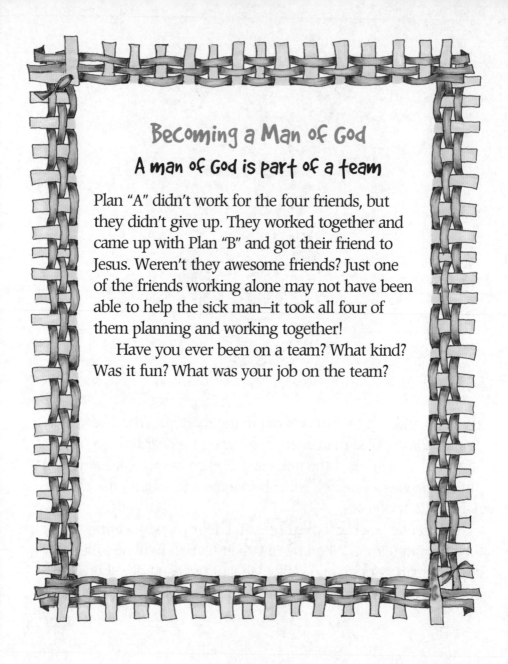

Becoming a Man of God
A man of God is part of a team

Plan "A" didn't work for the four friends, but they didn't give up. They worked together and came up with Plan "B" and got their friend to Jesus. Weren't they awesome friends? Just one of the friends working alone may not have been able to help the sick man—it took all four of them planning and working together!

Have you ever been on a team? What kind? Was it fun? What was your job on the team?

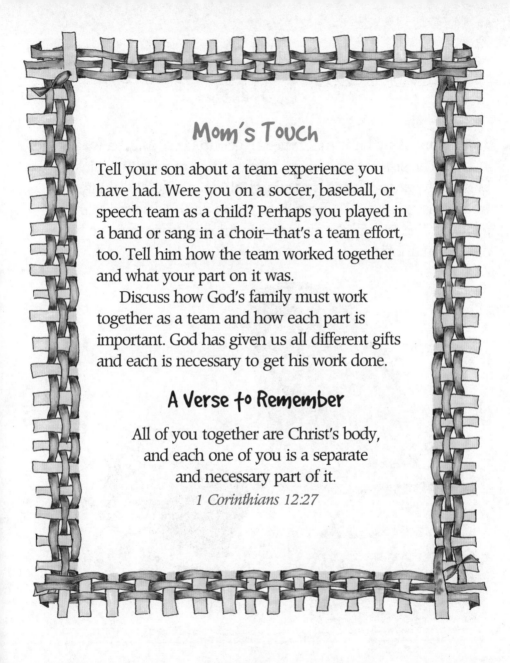

Mom's Touch

Tell your son about a team experience you have had. Were you on a soccer, baseball, or speech team as a child? Perhaps you played in a band or sang in a choir–that's a team effort, too. Tell him how the team worked together and what your part on it was.

Discuss how God's family must work together as a team and how each part is important. God has given us all different gifts and each is necessary to get his work done.

A Verse to Remember

All of you together are Christ's body,
and each one of you is a separate
and necessary part of it.

1 Corinthians 12:27

Devoted  Sisters

"Mary, it's your turn. Come on, get up now," Martha whispered. The sisters were taking turns sitting up with their sick brother, Lazarus. Martha sat through the night, gently laying cool, wet cloths on Lazarus's feverish forehead. In the daytime Mary gently fluffed his pillows and tried to think of ways to make him more comfortable.

Lazarus had been sick for several days, and Martha tried all the home remedies she knew. No matter what the worried sisters did, Lazarus got worse.

One afternoon when Mary went to town to buy food she heard that Jesus was in a nearby town. Mary ran all the way home to tell Martha. "Jesus is close by. Let's send for him. I know he can help Lazarus!" The sisters sent a message to Jesus right away. "Lazarus is very sick. Please come quickly!"

One day passed, then two . . . Mary and Martha waited eagerly for Jesus to come. Meanwhile, Lazarus's condition got worse and worse . . . then one night he quietly died.

"Why didn't Jesus come?" Mary asked through her tears. Martha sadly shook her head. She, too, wondered why Jesus hadn't come. She kept herself busy making arrangements for her brother's funeral, but her heart was confused and hurting.

A few days later a friend ran into the house and breathlessly reported, "Jesus is coming."

"Now he comes—when Lazarus is dead and buried. Where was Jesus when he could have helped my brother?" Martha dried her hands and went to meet Jesus. Her frustration spilled out at him. Mary couldn't believe how her prim and proper sister was speaking to the great teacher. "If you had been here, Lazarus wouldn't have died. That's the bottom line!"

Jesus wasn't upset at Martha. He asked, "Where is Lazarus buried?" They led him to the tomb, wondering what he was going to do. "Open the tomb!" Jesus commanded.

"No! Lazarus has been dead for four days; it will smell terrible in there!" Martha gasped.

But Jesus waited while the stone was moved; then he called, "Lazarus, come out!" Mary closed her eyes and hid behind Martha, until she heard "oohh" escape from her sister's lips. She looked up and saw Lazarus standing in the tomb door—alive and well!

Based on John 11:1-44

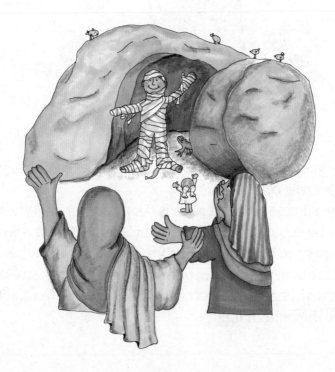

Becoming a Man of God
A man of God tells God how he feels

Mary and Martha told Jesus how they felt. They were disappointed and they didn't try to hide it. They knew that Jesus could take it. Jesus wants us to be honest with him; he knows our hearts anyway, so we might as well just tell him how we feel. We can tell him when we're disappointed or hurt. He won't stop loving us. Honesty is the best policy.

Have you ever been disappointed or sad about how God answered a prayer or handled a situation? Did you tell him?

Mom's Touch

Does your son feel he can be honest with you? If he feels he has been unjustly punished or accused, can he tell you?

Share a time from your childhood when you felt unjustly punished or accused. Did you tell your parents or teacher? What happened?

Talk about telling God your true feelings. Why is it scary to do that? Why is it OK to do so? Does God know how we feel anyway? Pray together and thank God that you can be honest with one another and with him.

A Verse to Remember

The LORD is close to all who call on him.

Psalm 145:18

A DARK DAY IN HISTORY

Mary's face flushed red and little beads of sweat popped out on her forehead. She felt a faintness creeping up from her stomach to her head so she grabbed a friend's arm to steady herself.

When a Roman soldier slapped a whip across Jesus' back, Mary flinched. She moved to the back of the crowd but kept her eyes on Jesus. "Get moving!" the soldier shouted. Jesus hoisted the wooden cross to his shoulder and walked slowly down the road.

Mary's heart ached as the crowds of people shouted at her son and made fun of him: "Yeah, look at the King of the Jews now!" "Why don't you call an angel army to save you?" She looked away. It was just too heartbreaking to see what they were doing to Jesus.

The gruesome parade reached the hill called
Calvary, and the soldiers threw Jesus to the
ground and nailed his hands and feet to the
wooden cross. When they dropped the
cross into the ground, Mary pushed her
way to the front, standing right below
Jesus. Jeers rang out, "Come on King
of the Jews. Save yourself. Where's all your
power now?"

The man on the cross was kind and loving. Mary had known him for his whole life and he had never done anything wrong or even unkind. Mary also remembered almost thirty-four years ago when the angel told her that she was going to have a baby and that he would be the Messiah—the one who would save his people. This must be what the angel meant.

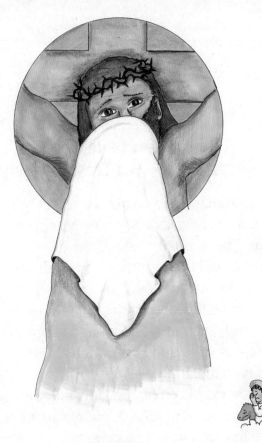

Mary looked into Jesus' eyes—the eyes of her son—the eyes of God's Son. Despite all the terrible things happening to him this day his eyes were filled with love, complete and total love, even for the people killing him and making fun of him.

It was the oddest feeling for Mary when Jesus lifted his head and said, "It is finished." When he died, part of her heart died too . . . and yet she knew she was reborn at that moment . . . into the family of God.

Based on John 19:16-30

Becoming a Man of God

A man of God understands Jesus died on the cross for him

A loving momma would do almost anything to help her son. But, there wasn't anything Mary could do about this. This was why Jesus came to earth. Jesus left the riches of heaven to come to earth and live as a poor man. He was not treated very nicely by some people. They finally killed him on the cross, just like a plain old thief, even though he hadn't done anything wrong. He was willing to go through all of this because he loves us so much.

Have you ever been blamed for something you didn't do? Did you just take the punishment or loudly announce that you were innocent?

Mom's Touch

Tell your son about a time when he was sick or hurt and how bad you felt for him.

Before Jesus died on the cross, people had to sacrifice an animal, such as a sheep or a dove, to God before they could ask him to forgive their sins. Explain to your son that we don't have to do that anymore because Jesus died on the cross as the sacrifice for our sins. Thank him for this wonderful gift!

A Verse to Remember

Christ died for everyone.

2 Corinthians 5:14

The Empty Tomb

The sun was just peeking over the horizon when three women began a quiet walk to the cemetery. Each woman walked with her head bowed, shoulders slumping. All of their hope had died when Jesus died. Their world turned upside down that day. Jesus taught them so much about God, but then he died—could they believe anything he said? Each woman felt a dull aching pain in her stomach.

Did the sun come up today? Was the sky still blue? Were flowers still colorful and sweet? You wouldn't know by looking at any of these women. Even in the middle of their pain the women wanted to do the right thing—that's what they had been taught their whole lives. So, they were going to anoint Jesus' body with oil and perfumes because that was their custom. But their hearts didn't feel anything except empty numbness.

The women had known each other for years, shared joys and sorrows, prayed together, but today none of them knew what to say. So, they walked in silence until one of them remembered the big stone. Several soldiers had strained and pushed to roll it in front of the tomb door. "How are we going to move that stone?" the woman wondered aloud. Her friend dropped the basket she was carrying. "How much more do we have to go through before this is all over?" she spouted in frustration.

"Come on, we'll figure something out," the third woman encouraged. As they rounded the bend before the tomb, the woman in front suddenly stopped. Her friends, walking with bowed heads, bumped right into her.

"It's . . . gone!" she whispered. "The stone is gone, and the tomb is open." The women looked at each other as fear rose in their throats. What could this mean?

The bravest of the three women stumbled into the open tomb. She fell to her knees when a voice said, "I know you're looking for Jesus. He's not here. He is alive. He came back to life just as he said he would."

"He's alive! He's alive!" the woman shouted to her friends. "Praise God! Praise God! Jesus is alive!"

Based on Mark 16:1-7

Becoming a Man of God

A man of God knows God will do what he says

The poor women going to the tomb were so sad they didn't know what to do. That's because they had forgotten what Jesus said he would do—or they didn't believe it. Jesus said he would come back to life, but they sure weren't expecting it when they went to the tomb that morning.

Has someone ever told you that something would happen, but you didn't believe it? If it did happen, how did you feel? If it didn't, how did you feel?

Mom's Touch

Share some of your hopes for your son's future. Share some of the hopes you had as a child. Did any of them come true?

Explain that the women at the tomb that morning had given up hope because they didn't know that Jesus would do what he said. When they found out he was alive and that he had done what he said, they were very, very happy. Thank Jesus for coming back to life and that you can someday be in heaven with him.

A Verse to Remember

You are looking for Jesus, the Nazarene,
who was crucified. He isn't here!
He has been raised from the dead!

Mark 16:6

No Leg to Stand On

Every day was the same for the man. His friends carried him to the same place near the Beautiful Gate of the city of Jerusalem. Sometimes they complained about having to take him there. On those days, they dropped him off quickly, then ran before he could ask them to do anything else. Crowds of people poured in and out of Jerusalem every day. He had a good spot for begging there by the Beautiful Gate.

Day in and day out the man begged money from the people going
in and out of Jerusalem. That's the only way he could earn any
money. His legs didn't work so he couldn't get a job. He was a pushy
man—that's why people sometimes didn't want to be around him. He
seemed to feel that healthy, strong men owed him something, and
he made it his purpose in life to get every cent from them that he
could.

This day started out like any other day . . . the trip to the Gate, his friends running away, his constant begging. "Come on—you can spare some change for a crippled old man!"

"Sir!" A voice interrupted the stream of begging. He looked up to see who was speaking to him, but the bright sun blinded him so that he couldn't make out the faces of the two men standing in front of him.

He waited for one of the men to drop coins into his metal cup; instead the same voice said, "I don't have any money to give you."

"Then move out of the way. Let the paying customers in." The beggar's voice dripped with sarcasm.

"Wait, I have something better than money," the voice said. The old man couldn't imagine anything better than money, but he was interested in what the stranger was talking about. So he waited. "In the name of Jesus of Nazareth, get up and walk!" the stranger said.

The man felt a strange tingling in his legs and feet. He had never felt ANYTHING in his legs and feet. Dead muscles zoomed to life, crooked bones straightened. Peter took the man's arms and lifted him to his feet. His legs held him up! Joy and gratitude flooded through his body and spilled from his mouth. "Praise God! Praise God!" he shouted, running, and jumping, and kicking his heels together.

Based on Acts 3:1-10

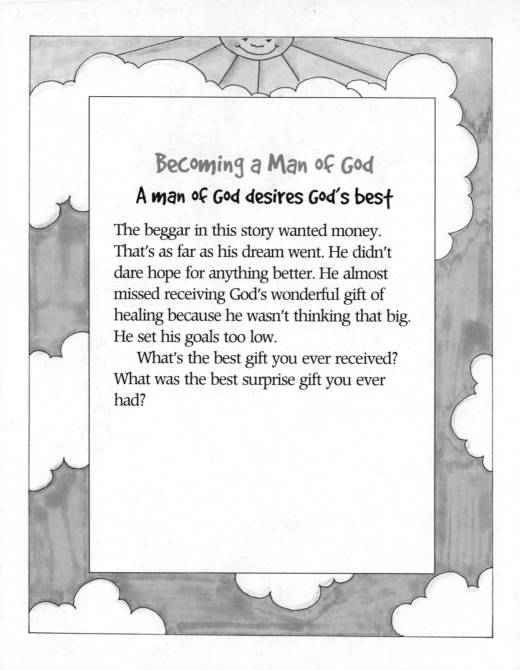

Becoming a Man of God

A man of God desires God's best

The beggar in this story wanted money. That's as far as his dream went. He didn't dare hope for anything better. He almost missed receiving God's wonderful gift of healing because he wasn't thinking that big. He set his goals too low.

What's the best gift you ever received? What was the best surprise gift you ever had?

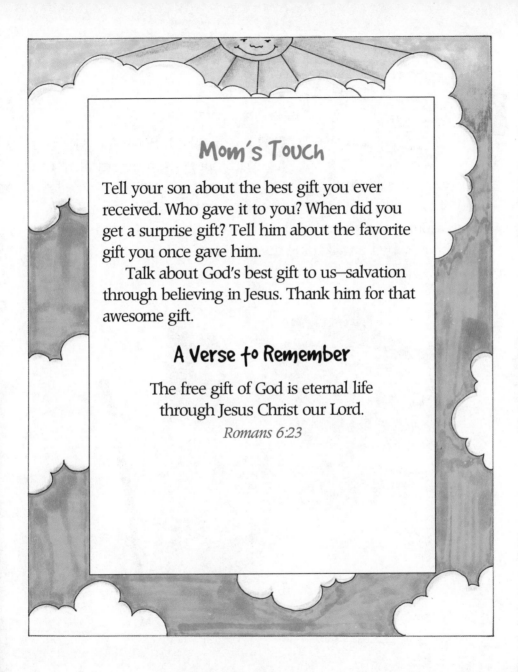

Mom's Touch

Tell your son about the best gift you ever received. Who gave it to you? When did you get a surprise gift? Tell him about the favorite gift you once gave him.

Talk about God's best gift to us—salvation through believing in Jesus. Thank him for that awesome gift.

A Verse to Remember

The free gift of God is eternal life through Jesus Christ our Lord.

Romans 6:23

"**P**hilip, go south down the desert road that goes from Jerusalem to Gaza." Philip didn't even question the order–when the angel of God tells you to do something, it's best to just do it! He turned around and started walking toward Gaza, even though he didn't know why he was going there.

After a while a fancy carriage came barreling toward him. Philip
stepped off the road so it wouldn't hit him. As it passed he saw
that a man from Ethiopia was inside. *He must be important in
the government judging from the markings on his carriage*, Philip
thought. The carriage was a good way down the road when the Holy
Spirit told Philip to run along beside it. Again, Philip didn't question,
he just broke into a fast run and caught up to the fancy chariot.
Running along beside it, he heard the man inside reading from the
book of Isaiah.

"Do you understand what you're reading?" Philip called to the man. The Ethiopian was surprised that a man was jogging along beside his chariot.

"No," he answered. "How can I understand it unless someone explains it to me? Are you saying that you understand it?"

"Well, yes. I can tell you what it means." So the man stopped his carriage and Philip climbed in.

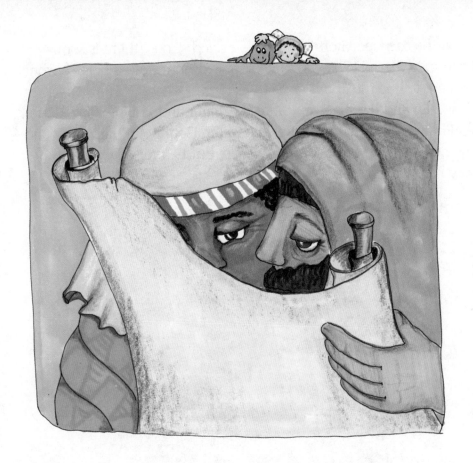

"These verses are talking about Jesus of Nazareth," Philip explained.
He used other verses he knew too, about why Jesus came to earth,
how he was killed but came back to life, and that he lives in
heaven and is making a way for all who believe in him to come to
heaven someday. Philip told the Ethiopian the whole story of God's
wonderful love.

"Stop the carriage! Stop!" the man shouted. "Look, there is some water over there. Why can't I be baptized right now? I believe what you are telling me about Jesus."

Philip and the man went into the water and Philip baptized him. As Philip lifted the man out of the water, God took Philip away and the new believer never saw him again, but he praised God all the way back to Ethiopia.

Based on Acts 8:26-40

Becoming a Man of God

A man of God shares God's love with others

Philip had information that would help the man in the chariot understand God's Word. He was willing to share that information even though he had to change his plans to talk to the man.

Who explains God's Word to you? Have you shared God's Word with anyone?

Mom's Touch

Tell your son about a favorite Sunday school teacher or pastor from your youth. Why did you like this person so much? Did you learn about God's Word from this person? Did your mom or dad share God's Word with you?

Ask your son if there is anything about God's Word that he doesn't understand. If so, talk about it or make plans to discuss it with your pastor together.

A Verse to Remember

Your word is a lamp for my feet
and a light for my path.
Psalm 119:105

A Changed ♥ Heart

"Christians! I hate them!" Every time Saul even said the word "Christian" he got a bad taste in his mouth and a knot of hate formed in his stomach. "I'm getting rid of all Christians if it's the last thing I do!" Just about the only thing that brought a smile to Saul's face was standing outside the jail and making fun of the Christians he had thrown in there.

After years of hunting down Christians and throwing them in jail, Saul felt he had taken care of all the Christians in Jerusalem.

"My work here is done. I think I'll go to Damascus and get rid of the Christians there, too." Saul and some of his friends began the walk to Damascus. Shortly after they began the trip, Saul heard a voice say, "Saul, why are you persecuting me?" He stopped and looked around but didn't see anyone.

"Saul, why are you persecuting me?" This time a blinding light shot out of the sky and shined directly on Saul. He fell to the ground and crawled on his hands and knees trying to get away from the light. But the light moved right along with him and the voice kept asking, "Saul, why are you persecuting me?"

For once, Saul's know-it-all friends were speechless. They heard the voice but couldn't figure out where it came from. Wisely, they didn't try to tell Saul what to do.

Finally Saul understood that whoever was speaking was not going away. "Who are you?" Saul asked softly. He wasn't sure he wanted to know.

"I am Jesus, the one you are persecuting."

Saul hung his head. *It's true then,* he thought. *Jesus is real. The Christians have been right all along. I'm the one who has been wrong.* Right there on the dusty road to Damascus Saul told Jesus he was sorry for everything he had done.

In that instant, Saul's heart was changed. He no longer wanted to hurt Christians; now he was a Christian, too. God changed Saul's name to Paul. Saul's life was devoted to getting rid of Christians—Paul's life was devoted to winning people to Christ.

Based on Acts 9

Becoming a Man of God
A man of God gives his whole life to God

Paul was a pretty bad guy before he believed in Jesus. He tried to hurt Christians and liked putting them in jail. But, after he believed in Jesus, Paul devoted his whole life to telling others about God. Paul didn't do things halfway. He gave 100% to whatever he did.

What do you give most of your energy to? Do you think about living for God or sharing his love with others every day? Is that something you think about only on Sunday?

Mom's Touch

Mom, share your conversion experience with your son. What were you like before meeting Jesus? How were you different afterwards? Tell him how living for God is part of your everyday life. Does he know if you pray daily, or have daily devotions? Does he hear you speak of God daily?

Pray together that you will both make God part of your lives every single day.

A Verse to Remember

Draw close to God,
and God will draw close to you.

James 4:8

Shake and Break

The jailer shoved Paul into the damp, dark cell. It was buried in the very center of the prison. Roaches and ants scurried across the floor as Paul fell onto it.

Paul had been in prison before, but this time he and Silas were in big trouble. The jailer had strict orders to be sure they didn't escape.

All I did was set a young girl free from the demon that controlled her, Paul thought. *You'd think people would thank me for saving her.* Instead Paul and Silas were beaten with sticks and whips, then thrown into prison. Paul remembered not so long ago when he made it his business to beat Christians with whips and chains. He had thrown them in prison and laughed that they would never see the light of day again.

Now, he and Silas sat on the filthy floor with their feet in chains. "You know, Silas, the other prisoners here need to know that God loves them," Paul said.

"Right, and we have a captive audience," Silas agreed. They began singing songs of praise to God. At first the other prisoners thought they were crazy; then they began to listen to the words Paul and Silas sang.

Many men leaned back against damp walls and listened to the comforting songs. Around midnight the walls and floor of the prison started shaking, almost like a large army was riding into town. Then the shaking got worse and Paul and Silas held onto each other. The floor lurched sideways and Paul was tossed across the room. The chains on his legs broke off. He was free! A grinding crack broke through the screams as the cell doors splintered and broke open. Prisoners started to run away, sure that the earthquake was their ticket to freedom.

The jailer struggled through piles of stones and broken chains to see his jail completely destroyed. Thinking all his prisoners were gone he drew his sword to take his own life. "Stop!" Paul shouted. "Don't hurt yourself. We're all here."

The jailer couldn't believe that Paul and Silas kept all the prisoners there when they all could have escaped. "Sir," he asked, "can you tell me how to be saved?"

Based on Acts 16:16-40

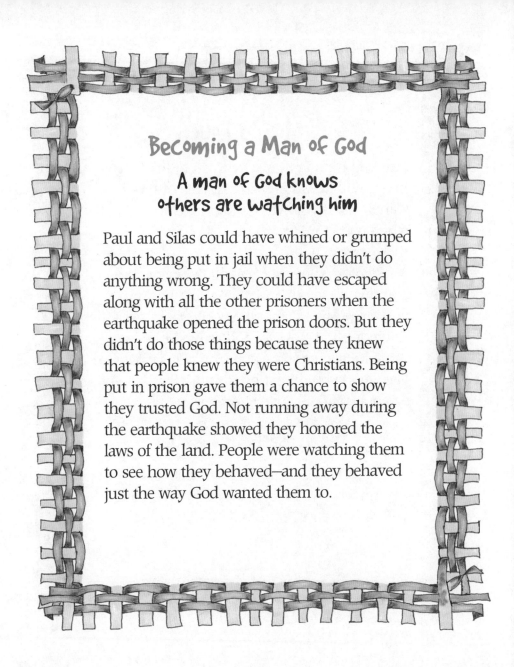

Becoming a Man of God

A man of God knows others are watching him

Paul and Silas could have whined or grumped about being put in jail when they didn't do anything wrong. They could have escaped along with all the other prisoners when the earthquake opened the prison doors. But they didn't do those things because they knew that people knew they were Christians. Being put in prison gave them a chance to show they trusted God. Not running away during the earthquake showed they honored the laws of the land. People were watching them to see how they behaved—and they behaved just the way God wanted them to.

Mom's Touch

Can you recall a time when you didn't behave in a way that was a good example of how God wants you to behave? Can you recall a time when you did? How did you feel after each of these experiences?

Reinforce your son's good behaviors by pointing them out and telling him how proud you are of him. Point out specific behaviors such as kindness or honesty and remind him how those behaviors show non-Christians what God is like. Remind him that he isn't too young to be an example of God's love to others.

A Verse to Remember

Be an example to all believers
in what you teach, in the way you live,
in your love, your faith, and your purity.

1 Timothy 4:12

Shipwreck!

"I demand to go to Rome! I am a Roman citizen and I have a right to be tried by Caesar himself." Paul was very firm about what he wanted. He knew that he had done nothing wrong and there was no real reason for his arrest. The only complaint against him was that he was a Christian and preached about Jesus Christ. He had a better chance for a fair trial in Rome than he did in Caesarea.

"Move it!" The guard jabbed his spear at the line of prisoners filing onto the big sailing ship. Chained together the prisoners couldn't move too quickly, but the guard paid no attention to that problem. "I said to get going!" The crack of his whip against some poor man's back made all the prisoners try their best to move a little faster.

One morning a strong wind blowing across the sea
sent the sailors into a panic. "Storm coming!
Batten down the hatches; tie down the cargo!
Move it!" Whips cracked across prisoners' backs
as they pushed to get set for the storm.
Paul heard the sailors' panic: "This is a
northeaster if I've ever seen one! We're taking on
water. The ship is going to go down!"

The prisoners bailed water as fast as their chains
would allow them to move, but the ship
kept sinking lower and lower in
the water. "Lighten her
load. Throw over the
cargo. Throw anything
that's loose!" Days at a time
the sailors bailed water and fought the storm, not
even taking time to eat.

"Stop worrying!" Paul shouted over the wind. "Go eat something. Most of you haven't eaten for two weeks. You've got to keep your strength up! God told me in a dream that the ship will sink. But, we will all be saved. Trust him!"

The other prisoners and the sailors thought Paul was crazy . . . and they kept right on bailing water. Later the ship hit some rocks and broke into a million pieces, but every man on the ship— prisoners, sailors, guards—made it safely to shore, just as God said they would.

Based on Acts 27:13-44

Becoming a Man of God
A man of God stays calm in a crisis

Everyone on the ship was going crazy except Paul. The sailors and prisoners all thought they were going to die. But Paul trusted God, and God said that he would take care of everyone on the ship.

What kinds of things make you afraid or nervous? Do you relax if your mom tells you everything will be OK, or do you keep on worrying?

Mom's Touch

Does your son know that you are sometimes nervous or afraid? Tell him what kinds of situations worry you. Tell him how you handle those fears and how you give them to God and trust him to take care of them.

Talk about your son's fears and encourage him to trust God with them. Memorize verses that remind him of God's care. Encourage him to say the verses or sing choruses about God's love and care when he is afraid.

A Verse to Remember

Give all your worries and cares to God,
for he cares about what happens to you.

1 Peter 5:7

An Evil Plan

"Listen to me! I've got nothing to apologize for. I've tried to live my life the way God wants me to! I am on trial just because I believe that we can live in heaven someday." Paul always said exactly what he thought. But, this speech to the High Council made the religious leaders angry. Suddenly a fight broke out between the Pharisees who agreed with Paul and the Sadducees who didn't.

"He's wrong!" some shouted.

"He's right!" others screamed.

The man in charge thought the men were going to rip Paul into pieces. "Put Paul in prison!" he shouted. "Otherwise these men will kill him!"

The next morning a group of more than forty Jews held a secret meeting. "We promise that we will not eat or drink until Paul is dead!"

"He is going down! We will have the leaders bring him back to the Council for more questions. On the way there will be a mysterious ambush—and Paul will be dead. Is everybody in?"

"Yeah! Right! We're in!" Cries rang out and fists shook in the air.

The group didn't know that a young boy stood outside the doorway of their secret meeting room. He heard their whole evil plan.

The boy quietly slipped away from the door and ran to the prison. Outside one tiny cell window he knelt on the ground. "Uncle Paul, Uncle Paul," he called. Paul came to the window, glad to see his nephew. The young boy told his uncle about the plan to kill him. Paul knew what to do.

"Sir," Paul called to one of the prison officials. "Please take this boy to the commander. He has important information that the commander needs to know."

The young boy wished his uncle would just tell the man about the plan. *It's too scary to talk to the commander. I'm just a kid*, he thought. But, he knew that his uncle's life depended on his courage. So, he went to the commander and shyly told him about the Jews' plans—and even how he was part of it because they wanted him to send Paul back to the High Council for questioning.

The commander listened to the boy's story, asked a few questions, then leaped into action. "Get two hundred soldiers ready to leave for Caesarea tonight. Also two hundred spearmen and seventy horsemen. Get horses for Paul to ride and take this letter to Governor Felix. Paul must be in Caesarea by morning!"

The young boy felt proud that he helped save Paul's life and ruined the evil plans of the hungry, thirsty Jews.

Based on Acts 23:1-35

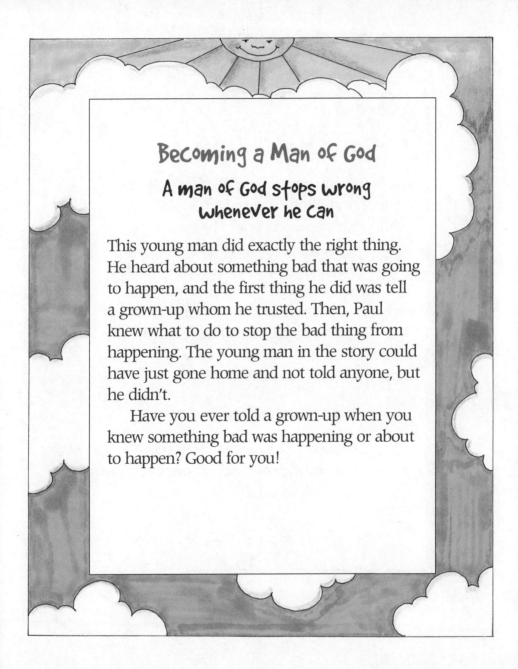

Becoming a Man of God

A man of God stops wrong whenever he can

This young man did exactly the right thing. He heard about something bad that was going to happen, and the first thing he did was tell a grown-up whom he trusted. Then, Paul knew what to do to stop the bad thing from happening. The young man in the story could have just gone home and not told anyone, but he didn't.

Have you ever told a grown-up when you knew something bad was happening or about to happen? Good for you!

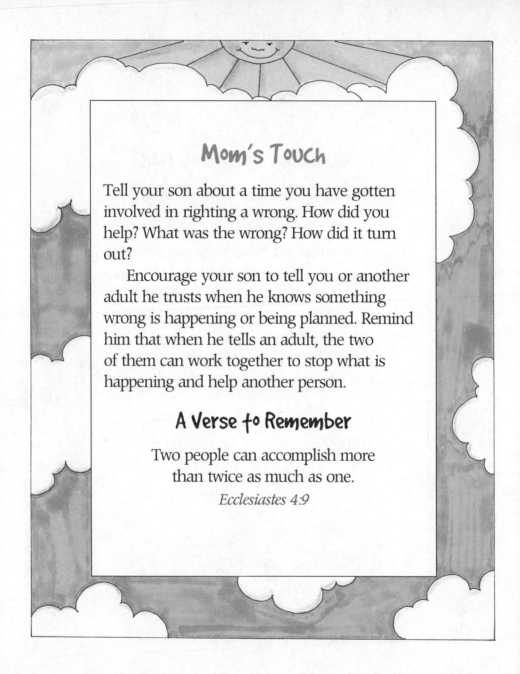

Mom's Touch

Tell your son about a time you have gotten involved in righting a wrong. How did you help? What was the wrong? How did it turn out?

Encourage your son to tell you or another adult he trusts when he knows something wrong is happening or being planned. Remind him that when he tells an adult, the two of them can work together to stop what is happening and help another person.

A Verse to Remember

Two people can accomplish more
than twice as much as one.

Ecclesiastes 4:9

The Holy  City

The apostle John was a friend of Jesus. He traveled with him, and heard him teach, and saw him do amazing miracles. He also saw Jesus die on the cross. Jesus asked John to take care of his mother, Mary. John loved Jesus—and Jesus loved John.

When John was an old man God sent an angel with a special message for all people who love God. John wrote it down in a special book called Revelation. This is part of John's message:

The old world full of bad people and bad things will disappear someday. A new city will come down from heaven, and God's people will live in it with him. This city will be more beautiful than anything you can imagine. It will sparkle like diamonds on a sunny day. Walls that are wide and tall will surround the whole city.

Each side of the wall will have three gates in it. Each gate is named for one of the twelve tribes of Israel, and a beautiful angel will stand guard at each gate.

The wall of this beautiful city will have twelve big foundation stones, one named for each of Jesus' special friends, the disciples.

The city will be made of pure gold—gold that is as clear as glass. The foundation stones of the wall will each have beautiful gemstones in them like emerald, onyx, topaz, and amethyst. The twelve gates will be made of pearls—big, big pearls. Each gate will be one single pearl!

There will be no need for a sun or moon in this beautiful city, because God's light will fill it. Nothing bad will be allowed inside; no sadness will be there either.

John wrote about the holy city so that God's children can look forward to being there someday–with Jesus and with everyone who loves him!

Based on Revelation 21

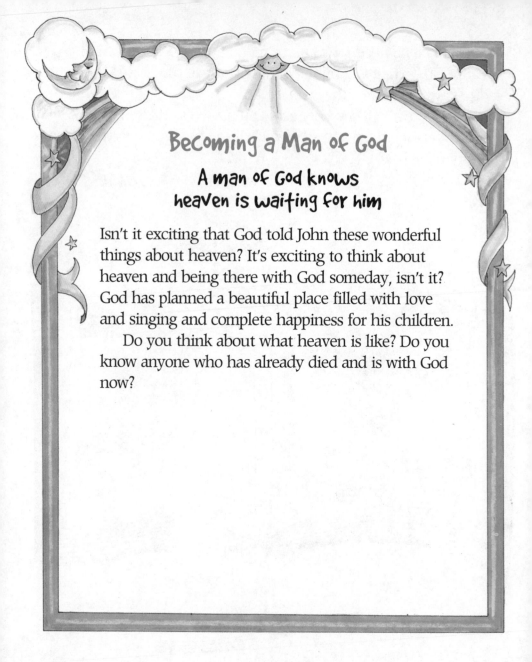

Becoming a Man of God

A man of God knows heaven is waiting for him

Isn't it exciting that God told John these wonderful things about heaven? It's exciting to think about heaven and being there with God someday, isn't it? God has planned a beautiful place filled with love and singing and complete happiness for his children.

Do you think about what heaven is like? Do you know anyone who has already died and is with God now?

Mom's Touch

Tell your son about loved ones who have already died and whom you will see again in heaven someday. Talk about rewards and how rewards are given for jobs done well—winning a race means you get a ribbon or trophy; studying hard for a test means you get a good grade. Heaven is a wonderful reward for God's children. Ask your son what he thinks heaven will be like.

Pray together and thank God for heaven and for making a way for us to be with him there.

A Verse to Remember

All who are victorious will inherit all these blessings, and I will be their God, and they will be my children.

Revelation 21:7

Part 2

Stories
for Fathers
and Sons

Dear Dads,

The relationship a little boy has with his dad is so important. A good relationship helps establish a good self-image and self-confidence. Most little boys think their dads can do absolutely anything. Dad has a unique ability to teach his son the truths of the Bible and how to apply Scripture to life.

The *Little Boys Bible Storybook* provides an opportunity to look at well-loved Bible stories through the eyes and hearts of the Bible characters who lived them. We don't really know how these people felt about the experiences they lived through. But, they were people like we are, so we can imagine how they felt. By thinking about how these people may have felt, we can learn lessons of how to apply Scripture to our lives and how to make God real in every aspect of life.

Caron Turk has once again hidden a little angel in each illustration. I know that you and your little boy will have fun looking for this little angel. Hopefully, you'll be able to discuss the Bible story as you do your angel search. Caron and I pray that this book will provide hours of "together time" and entertainment with a purpose for you and your son. We pray that you will grow closer together and that both you and your son will go deeper in your relationship with the Lord through reading and talking about this book.

God bless,

Carolyn Larsen

How It All Began

"You're a bear. You look like a . . . rabbit. Hmm, I'll call you a turtle." Adam took the job of naming the animals very seriously. God was trusting him to do a good job. "Wow, you sure made a lot of animals, God. How did you think of so many different kinds?" Adam asked, taking a break. Thinking up names was hard work.

"I'm glad you asked. Let me tell you how this world came to be," God answered.

"In the beginning, not a star twinkled, not a bird sang, not a bug crawled. Everything was dark and quiet and empty," God said.

"Sounds kind of boring," Adam whispered.

"Exactly. So I said, 'Let there be light!' and light exploded into the darkness. I made day and night and earth and sky. Then I filled the land with every kind of plant I could think of . . . trees, bushes, flowers, grass, and . . ."

"That must have taken a long time," Adam interrupted.

"Not really, that took only three days."

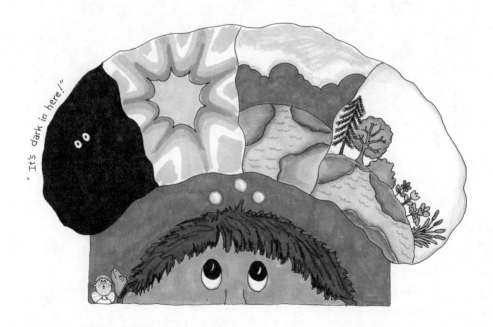

"It's dark in here!"

"Three days, wow." Adam was amazed. "What did you do next?"

"The fourth day is one of my favorites." God smiled. "I sprinkled stars in the night sky, made the bright sun to light the day, and the gentle moon to light the night."

"All that in one day? You were certainly busy!" Adam was impressed.

"The fifth day I noticed how empty the oceans were . . . so I filled them with fish and dolphins, octopus and eels, all kinds of things that swim."

"It must have been fun to think of all those things," Adam said. "I like to watch dolphins jumping out of the water. When did you make the birds?"

"On that very same day. From big bald eagles to tiny hummingbirds, I filled the sky with all kinds of things that fly."

"The sixth day started off with animals. Big lions, soft rabbits . . . any animal I could think of. When I finished making animals, I turned my attention to you," God continued.

"Me?" Adam didn't know what to think.

"Yes, I made you, Adam, to be able to think and make decisions. You can love and care for others. You are a lot like me."

"Wow, that's awesome. What did you do next?" Adam wondered.

"I looked around at all I had made and I liked everything I saw. I knew I had done my very best. So, on the seventh day, I took a rest," God said.

Based on Genesis 1

Becoming a Man of God
A man of God is made in God's image

God had some wonderful ideas, didn't he? He thought of all kinds of unusual animals—some are funny looking and some are kind of scary. He even made animals that make nice pets for us. He also thought of all kinds of flowers with hundreds of different colors and scents.

But, God's best creation . . . the one he saved for last . . . was people! He made people to be a lot like him. We can think and make decisions and learn the difference between right and wrong. He even gave that first person a job to do. He trusted Adam to name all the animals, and he asked Adam and Eve to take care of the Garden of Eden.

You are made in God's image, too. He made you the way you are . . . with a kind heart and jolly laugh. He gave you interests in sports or science or carpentry, or whatever you like to do. Be happy with who you are! Learn more about the interests and talents that God gave you and how you can use them to help other people.

Dad's Turn

Share with your son a memory about things you liked to do when you were a little boy. Did you enjoy fishing with your dad or helping your grandfather build things? Maybe you loved making cookies with your mom. Does your son have any of the same interests that you had as a child?

It's so important for your son to know how proud you are of him. Point out things about him that you appreciate . . . his kindness, sense of humor, helpfulness. Then remind him of the activities you and he enjoy doing together. Tell him how special he is to you . . . and to God!

A Verse to Remember

God created people in his own image;
God patterned them after himself;
male and female he created them.

Genesis 1:27

Water Works

"Your feet stink; get them out of my face!" Japheth shouted.

"Oh yeah, well your breath stinks; don't breathe on my feet!" Ham shouted back at his little brother.

"Be quiet!" Shem moaned. "Every bone in my body aches and you two just interrupted my last few minutes of sleep! I know it's a good thing that Dad is building the big boat, but it sure is hard work."

After the three brothers finished breakfast they went out
to help their dad. He was building a boat, the biggest boat
anyone had ever seen. God told him to build it because a
great-big-earth-cleaning flood was coming. God was tired of
the way people lived—only thinking about themselves—evil
and selfish and paying no attention to God. Everyone except
their dad, Noah. He obeyed God; that's why God warned him
about the flood.

When the boat was finished, the boys happily went back to their old chores, which seemed pretty easy now. One day Japheth was playing outside when he noticed something strange. "Dad, zillions of animals are marching straight toward the boat!"

Noah smiled. "God is sending two of every kind of animal to go in the boat. He wants them to be safe, too. Then, after the flood, they will have babies so there will be animals on earth again."

A few days later Noah cried, "Grab your carry-ons, boys, it's time to get in the boat." Soon they heard raindrops pounding on the roof. It rained so long that the whole earth flooded. All the people died . . . except the Noah family, safe inside the boat. One morning, forty days after the first raindrop fell, Shem shushed his noisy brothers. "Listen!" But they didn't hear anything. "I know . . . it's quiet! The rain has finally stopped! Yahoo!" The brothers cheered because their stinky boat ride (after all, it was full of animals!) would soon be over.

"Calm down." Noah smiled. "God will tell us when to leave. There's still lots of water out there." At least once a day someone asked, "Is it time yet?" Finally, one day they all came out of the boat to a clean new world.

Noah called everyone together. "See that rainbow in the sky? That shows God's promise to us that he will never send such a big flood again. Let's take time to thank him." Then the whole family (and maybe a few smart animals) knelt and thanked God for his love and protection.

Based on Genesis 6-9

Becoming a Man of God
A man of God obeys God

The Noah boys grew up in a family that loved and honored God. The whole family probably took some heavy teasing from friends and neighbors when their dad started building the big boat. But, the boys knew that their father would always choose to obey God, even when that wasn't the easy or popular thing to do. Since he did obey, those in the Noah family were the only people left on earth after the big flood. The first thing Noah led his family to do after they got off the smelly boat was to take time to thank God for his love and protection.

You know that the right thing to do is obey God, obey your parents, obey teachers. But sometimes, that isn't the easy thing to do. When was a time that you obeyed and you were glad you did? When was a time when you didn't obey and you were sorry later?

Dad's Turn

When you're a kid, sometimes it seems like someone is always telling you what to do. Obeying can get pretty old. Tell your son about a time when you obeyed, even though it was difficult. Were you later glad you obeyed? Now, tell him about a time when you didn't obey, because it was hard to or because your friends wanted you to do something different. Were you sorry you disobeyed? What happened?

Obeying God can be extra hard if your friends don't care anything about him. Encourage your son to do the right thing even if his friends want him to do something else. Remind him to always obey . . . and to remember to thank God for his love and care.

A Verse to Remember

Those who obey God's word
really do love him.

1 John 2:5

Huh? What Did You Say?

There once was a time when every person on earth spoke the same language. No matter where a person went he could ask, "How do I get to the store?" or, "How are your kids doing?" It was wonderful! Everyone could talk to everyone else. But then . . .

"Hey, you guys. I've got a super idea!" someone said. "Why don't we build a new city? Look, I've already drawn up some plans. It will be the biggest, most beautiful city ever." People hurried to look at the drawings and everyone agreed to work together and build a city that would be better than anything else ever built.

The people got right to work. Some made bricks and others stacked the bricks into walls. Some dug holes to be the foundations of the buildings. It was hard work! One day someone said, "What our city needs is a big, big tower . . . so high that it reaches the sky! Then everyone in the rest of the world will know how smart and powerful we are."

THE TOWER

But, the smart and powerful people forgot all about God! He was sad to hear the way they were talking. They thought they were so smart and powerful that they didn't even need him anymore. "They think they are so great, but they are leaving me completely out," God said. "How can I get their attention again?" Then, God came up with a plan.

The next morning one workman said, "Toss me that brick!"
But, his buddies couldn't understand him! "Huh? What did
he say?" someone asked . . . but no one could understand
that man either! Everyone was speaking different languages!
People quickly looked around for people they could
understand. Pretty soon everyone divided into groups with
people who spoke the same way. The big tower and the fancy
city were completely forgotten . . . but God wasn't!

Based on Genesis 11:1–9

Becoming a Man of God
A man of God glorifies God, not himself

What were these guys thinking? This group of men got so caught up in their fancy building that they completely forgot about God. They didn't think they even needed him anymore. Their grand ideas and fancy tower made them think they were very clever and important. They were shouting to the world, "Hurrah for me!" instead of "Hurrah for God!"

God took care of that attitude, didn't he? He knew that if they couldn't understand each other or communicate with each other, they wouldn't be able to work together on the tower. So, he created new languages. God wants people to realize they need him and to remember to give him the glory for whatever gifts and talents he gives them.

What kinds of things are you good at doing? Sports? Music? Reading? When you do those things do you enjoy having people tell you how great you are? Do you remember to thank God for those talents and gifts? Remember to glorify him in everything you do.

Dad's Turn

The men who built the Tower of Babel were pretty creative, weren't they? They were also pretty ambitious. What is the biggest, most challenging thing you've ever tackled? The problem with the people in the story was that they decided they didn't need God. They thought they could do something (build a big tower) that would make them powerful and important. They were glorifying themselves instead of God. Give your son an example of how to glorify God. What are the talents or gifts God has given you? How do you use those for God's glory?

Talk with your son about how important it is to glorify God by what we do . . . not ourselves. Suggest things you could do together on a daily basis—read a Bible story, pray together, talk about things God does for you every day. Suggest that your son can glorify God by the way he plays with his siblings, or treats God's creation. What are some other ways?

A Verse to Remember

Let us continually offer our sacrifice of praise to God by proclaiming the glory of his name.

Hebrews 13:15

Good News . . . Bad News

"So, how do you like it down there? You can stay there 'til you rot . . . don't feel so special now, do you?" Joseph's brothers were fed up with him. "Dad likes you best and he doesn't even try to hide it. He gives you fancy presents, like this coat, but does he ever have anything for us? Of course not! Then you have these unbelievable dreams that we're going to bow down to you—you're going to rule over us! Get over yourself, brother!"

Joseph's brothers were actually going to let him die in that hole! Just when he thought it was hopeless, Joseph heard them whispering to each other. Maybe they had changed their minds! "Yeah, I see them . . . slave traders, probably on the way to Egypt," he heard. "Not a bad idea. Yeah, I like it. We sell them the kid—tell Dad an animal killed him. He's out of our hair and we won't be guilty of murder. Best of all, Mr. 'I'm-so-important' will be a slave! Haa haaa haaa!" Joseph didn't like the way this was going.

"The bad news is, I'm a slave. The good news is, Potiphar liked me and put me in charge of his house. The bad news is, Mrs. Potiphar lied about me so now I'm in jail." Joseph had plenty of time to think about his situation. "Well, I'm going to keep on trusting God to take care of me. He hasn't let me down yet, so I'll keep praying to him, every day!"

"Are you feeling ill today, Sir?" Pharaoh's advisor asked.

"Not really, but I had nightmares last night and I couldn't sleep. I remember them, but I can't figure out what they mean," the Egyptian king answered.

"Sir, I've heard there is a young man in our prison who can explain dreams," the servant said.

Before he finished speaking, Pharaoh shouted, "Get him!" God helped Joseph explain Pharaoh's dreams. He was so happy that he made Joseph the second highest commander of the country!

A little while later, there was a terrible drought–no food would grow anywhere. But, God had warned Joseph about it and he stored up lots of food. People even came from other countries to buy some. One day, Joseph saw some men waiting to buy food. They didn't recognize him, but Joseph knew who they were! His own brothers–the ones who had sold him into slavery. He could have thrown them in jail, or even had them killed. But, he didn't. He said, "Hey, brothers, it's me, Joseph. I forgive you for trying to hurt me. I'm so glad to see you." That's exactly what God wanted Joseph to do!

Based on Genesis 37–45

Becoming a Man of God
A man of God forgives others

If anyone ever had a reason to be mad at someone, it was Joseph. His brothers did a very mean and spiteful thing to him. God took the things they meant to be bad and turned them into good for Joseph, because Joseph loved and trusted God.

Then when his brothers really needed to buy food from him, Joseph had a perfect opportunity for revenge. What a great chance to get even . . . but he didn't. Once again, the important thing to remember is that Joseph loved God and he knew that the right thing to do would be to forgive his brothers. That's what he did, and he showed a wonderful example of how God forgives his children for the wrong things we do.

Have you ever been really angry with someone who was mean to you? What did they do to you? Did you do something back to them? How did you feel afterward?

Dad's Turn

Share a memory with your son of a time when someone did something mean to you. How did you respond to that person? Did you get even with him or her? Now recall a time when you forgave someone's actions toward you instead of taking revenge.

This could come down to a discussion of what is "macho" versus what is godly. Teach your son that it isn't wimpy to forgive someone instead of getting even with them. In fact, it takes a bigger person to forgive without getting even.

Thank God together for this story that is an example of his forgiveness. Thank him for forgiving our sinful actions.

A Verse to Remember

Love your enemies.
Pray for those who persecute you.
Matthew 5:44

Mom's Good Plan

"No! Pharaoh and his creepy soldiers can't have my precious baby!" Jochebed stomped around the room holding the baby so tightly that a loud b-u-r-pppp popped from his lips.

"Honey, I love this baby as much as you, but Pharaoh ordered that all Hebrew baby boys be killed. We're just two lowly slaves; how are we going to stop it?" her husband asked in frustration.

Jochebed had already been thinking about how to save her son. A few days later she put her plan into action. "Miriam, hold your brother and try to keep him quiet," she ordered. Miriam watched in confusion as her mom raced out of the house. She returned a while later carrying an armload of reeds. Quickly, Jochebed wove the reeds into a little basket with a lid. Miriam couldn't figure out what her mom was planning to do.

"Come on, we're going down to the river," Jochebed announced, when the basket was finished. They slipped through back streets, hiding behind trees when they saw another person. When they reached the river, Jochebed said, "Give me the baby." She gently laid her little boy in the basket. Giving him one last kiss, she put the cover on and shoved the basket onto the water. "What happens to him now is in God's hands," she whispered.

Tears streamed down Jochebed's face while she walked home. Miriam hid at the edge of the river and watched her little brother's basket float away. It was moving close to where the Egyptian princess often came to bathe in the river. Sure enough, a few minutes later Miriam heard the laughter of the princess and her servants. *What if she sees the basket? Will she give the baby to her father? Will my brother be killed after all?* Miriam's heart pounded so hard that she was afraid the princess would hear it.

The princess spotted the basket immediately. "Bring it to me," she ordered. When they took the cover off, Miriam could hear her brother crying. "A Hebrew baby. Isn't he cute? I want to keep him," the princess announced.

Miriam bounded out of the grass before she could think about what she was doing. "Your highness, would you like a Hebrew woman to be his nurse?" The princess said yes and Miriam dashed home. "Momma, come quick. The princess is going to keep the baby and she wants someone to take care of him!"

Based on Exodus 2:1–10

Becoming a Man of God
A man of God does what he can

Jochebed could have just thrown her hands up in despair and said, "Oh well, I guess Pharaoh will kill my son." But, Jochebed wasn't like that. She loved her baby boy very much, and she was willing to do whatever she could to keep him alive. She used her brain to think up a plan, and she used the talents God gave her to make the basket. God blessed her efforts, and the little baby's life was saved.

There are times when the best thing we can do is pray and trust God with how a situation will turn out. But, there are also times when we should use our brains and the abilities God has given us to solve our problems. So when we have a problem to solve or a project to do we should pray for guidance and help, then . . . get busy!

When was a time you thought through how to solve a problem, then did it?

Dad's Turn

Give your son two examples—one of a situation where you came up with a plan to solve a problem, then put the plan into action. Perhaps this example would be of a larger situation, where you were part of a large group working to solve the problem. Next, give him an example of a situation where your hands were tied, and all you could do was pray and trust God with the solution. Tell him how both situations turned out.

Ask your son if there are any situations he is currently concerned about, such as homeless people in your city, or a friend at school who is having a hard time. Come up with a plan together for something you can do to help, then work on it together.

A Verse to Remember

Think of ways to encourage one another
to outbursts of love and good deeds.
Hebrews 10:24

A True Sign

Moses was shaking in his sandals.... well, he would have been if he were wearing sandals! In fact, he wanted to turn and run as far away from the burning bush as he could. But, God was in that bush (that's why it was burning), and Moses knew he couldn't run away from God.

"Moses, you're going to free my people from slavery," God
announced. "Tell the Israelites that I've put you in charge.
Then, go to the Pharaoh of Egypt and tell him that I said to
let my people go!"

"You've got the wrong guy," Moses whispered. "I'm just a shepherd. I take care of sheep, not people. Who would listen to me? Why would anyone believe that you put me in charge?" He was backing away from the bush a step at a time now.

"What have you got in your hand?" God asked.

Why does he all of a sudden care about my equipment? Moses wondered. "It's just my shepherd staff," he answered, holding it up for God to see.

"Throw it down on the ground," God said.

"What?"

"Throw it down," God said again. Moses tossed the staff in front of the bush.

Suddenly, it scooted right back at Moses . . . it had turned into a snake! Moses screamed and backed up so fast that he fell right down (if there was one thing he didn't like, it was snakes). "Pick it up by the tail," God ordered. Moses looked at the hissing snake. Then at the burning bush . . . snake . . . bush. Closing his eyes, he grabbed the snake's tail. Instantly, it was his staff again! It sort of sounded like God was smiling as he said, "Do this for the Israelites; then they will believe I sent you."

Based on Exodus 3:1-4:5

Becoming a Man of God
A man of God takes a chance

God had a lot of trust in Moses. He asked Moses to do a very big job . . . and God knew it wasn't going to be easy. Moses' job was taking care of sheep. He probably thought he would be a shepherd for the rest of his life. But, God had bigger plans. However, when God shared those plans with Moses, instead of leaping at the chance, Moses was scared! Being scared was OK, because God was asking him to do something new and something big. He should have been scared—but he should have also trusted God for help.

Moses took a little convincing, and God knew that the stick-to-snake thing would do the trick. So, it took Moses a little time, and he needed the help of a little miracle to realize that this was GOD talking to him. When he understood that, Moses left his sheep and took a chance. He obeyed God's request and trusted God to help him.

Have you ever been a little scared at something new you had to do? How did you get over being afraid?

Dad's Turn

Your son may look at you and think that you are never, ever afraid of anything. While that may make you feel cool, it would help him to know that sometimes you are afraid or nervous about things. Share a time when you have been afraid, especially of something new. Perhaps it was a time from your childhood when your family moved to a new town and you had to attend a new school. Maybe it was a big project at work that looked overwhelming to you. Or, maybe it was something you knew that God was asking you to do—go on a missions trip, or serve on a committee or board.

Explain how the situation turned out and what part your faith played in the outcome. Did you sense God's presence through this experience?

Ask your son if there are things in his life that frighten him. Are there things that he thinks could or might happen in the future that make him nervous? Remind him of the ways God has shown his presence to your family in the past and that these experiences show you can trust him for the future.

A Verse to Remember

My help comes from the LORD,
who made the heavens and the earth!

Psalm 121:2

"Let My People Go!"

"**W**hy did you come here? You've caused nothing but trouble. Asking Pharaoh to let us go made him mad. So now, he's made us work even harder! Why can't you just be quiet?" The angry people let Moses have it with both barrels! Moses just shook his head—he was only doing what God told him to do—and God had to talk him into it in the first place!

"God," Moses prayed, "you're going to have to do
something to show the Israelites and Pharaoh that
you mean business!" Well, that was certainly no
problem because God had a plan . . . all the water
in Egypt turned to blood! Egyptians could be heard
shouting, "What will we drink? The fish are all dead!
Yuck, it smells!" But did this miracle make Pharaoh
let the Israelites leave? Not on your life!

"Any more ideas, God?" Moses prayed
again. No problem—each time Moses
asked Pharaoh to let the people leave
Egypt and Pharaoh answered "NO!",
something terrible happened to the
Egyptians . . . frogs filled the land or
gnats bugged the people, then hail killed
their crops. On and on it went until nine
terrible, horrible things happened to the
Egyptians.

Each time some new plague hit, Pharaoh called Moses back to the palace and said, "OK, OK, OK, stop this plague and I'll let you take the people out of Egypt." But, every time God called off the plague, Pharaoh changed his mind again. Finally, after the ninth plague, the Egyptian people were getting sick of this. "Maybe Pharaoh should just let them go!" some Egyptians whispered to each other at the town well.

Meanwhile, the Israelites were discouraged and Moses was confused. "Didn't God say he was going to deliver us from Egypt? Why hasn't Pharaoh let us leave?" Moses did the only thing he could think of. He knelt down and poured out his heart to God: "Are my people going to die here? Are we always going to be slaves? O God, what's going on? Have you forgotten us?"

Of course, God had a plan. One more terrible, horrible thing would happen that would convince Pharaoh once and for all to let the Israelites go.

Based on Exodus 7:1-10:29

Becoming a Man of God
A man of God goes to God with his problems

Remember when God talked to Moses at the burning bush? He asked Moses to lead his people out of Egypt, so Moses knew that he was doing a job God had given him to do. So, why was it so hard? Moses may have wondered why the Pharaoh didn't just say, "Oh, you want to take the Israelites out of Egypt; OK, go ahead." After all, the whole thing was God's idea. But, just because a job comes from God doesn't mean it's going to be easy. Besides, not everyone cares what God says about things (Pharaoh, for example).

So, when the going got tough, Moses did the best thing he could possibly do—he talked to God about the problem. He told God how frustrated he was about the situation. He asked God what to do next, and he reminded God that he was trusting him for help.

What do you do when you have a problem? Who do you talk to about it? Has there been a time when you've prayed about a problem and then knew for sure that God helped you with it?

Dad's Turn

Your son will learn a lot about how to handle problems and difficulties by watching how you handle them. Does he know that you take your problems to God? What's the biggest problem or most difficult situation you remember facing as a child? Why was it so difficult? How did you handle it? Did you pray about it?

Can you share a time when you prayed diligently about something and saw God's hand in the solution? Did that make it easier to trust God the next time you had a problem? Remind your son that remembering how God has worked in the past makes it easier to trust him the next time. Remind him too, that when God gives you a job to do, he will always help you do it.

A Verse to Remember

God will surely do this for you,
for he always does just what he says.

1 Corinthians 1:9

follow That cloud!

G od had one
more terrible,
horrible miracle in mind
to convince Pharaoh to let
the Israelites leave Egypt. The
firstborn son in every Egyptian
home died—even Pharaoh's son. After
that, Pharaoh turned to Moses and
through his tears he whispered, "Get out
of Egypt!"

God came in a huge cloud and
led the people out of Egypt. At
night the cloud turned to fire. The
Israelites knew that God was leading
them.

"We'll camp here," Moses announced when they were near the Red Sea. Women made dinner as their children ran and played.

Things were fine until someone shouted, "What's that cloud of dust over there?"

"It's Pharaoh's army! He's changed his mind again and sent his soldiers to bring us back." In a split second the Israelites were all over Moses again. "Did you bring us out here to die? We should have stayed in Egypt!" What would Moses do now?

"Watch what God will do for you!" Moses shouted, climbing up on a rock. He held his big shepherd's staff out over the water, and a strong wind began to blow. The water of the Red Sea splashed and blew. The people squished together as they backed away from the sea. Mumbles of, "What's going on? What is he doing?" rolled through the crowd.

"God is saving you," Moses cried. The wind blew harder and harder, finally blowing the water into two big walls. The ground between the walls was . . . dry. There wasn't even a drop of mud.

What does this mean? the people wondered, staring at the water hallway.

"Go on through!" Moses cried. The frightened people held back until one man finally stepped out. The people followed him, eyeing the big water walls with wonder.

It took a long time for all the people to cross through the sea, even though they hurried as fast as they could. "The Egyptian army is following us into the sea," the Israelites screamed.

"Hurry through," Moses called to the last few people. Then he raised his hand over the sea again, and the water crashed over the soldiers and chariots. Every Egyptian soldier died in the Red Sea that day, but God kept every Israelite safe!

Based on Exodus 14

Becoming a Man of God
A man of God sticks with a job

Remember w-a-a-a-y back when God talked to Moses at the burning bush? That's when God told Moses to free the Israelites from slavery in Egypt. Remember how after Moses got to Egypt, the pharaoh wouldn't let the people go? And the people complained about Moses getting them in trouble with the pharaoh? Well, there may have been times when Moses wanted to give up and leave the people to their complaining, but he didn't. Moses stuck with the job God had given him. Moses decided to finish the job, and he didn't let problems and complaining stop him.

It's important to keep in mind that every time Moses or the people had a problem, every step of the way, Moses talked to God. He asked God's help and waited for God's leading. God and Moses were a great team!

Have you ever had a job to do that seemed too big for you? Maybe you had to clean your messy room, or maybe you had tons of homework, or perhaps you were supposed to help Dad rake leaves in the yard. Did you stick with the job until it was finished? Was it hard to do that?

Dad's Turn

Two lessons grow from this story—a good work ethic and dependence on God. Your son will learn a good work ethic by watching how you approach work. Children watch their parents, even when it doesn't seem like they are paying any attention, and both of these examples will be noticed.

Share a story with your son of a job you faced that seemed completely overwhelming. Tell him if you were tempted to quit before the job was finished. Tell him how you felt when the job was finished.

When was a time that you truly trusted God for help with a situation? How did God help you through this situation? Ask your son if he has anything facing him that seems overwhelming. Pray with him about the big job. Then, see if you can work out a schedule to help him take the job in small chunks and work through the entire situation.

A Verse to Remember

Those who wait on the LORD
will find new strength.
They will fly high on wings like eagles.
They will run and not grow weary.
They will walk and not faint.

Isaiah 40:31

Hard Water

Moses dug his shepherd's staff into the sand and pulled himself up the small hill. "I'm so tired, but I can't stop," he said. "God gave me the job of leading the Israelites out of Egypt, and time after time God has done miracles so the people would know that he's with us. Now thousands and thousands of men, women, and children are depending on me. I have to keep going."

"Wow, it's hot out here," someone said. "Yeah, the sun is beating down," someone else added. Pretty soon, everyone around Moses was complaining about the heat. "Why can't we stop and get a drink?" someone shouted from a few rows back. "A DRINK? Do you SEE any water around here?" the first man shouted back.

"We're in a lousy desert. There's no water. We're going to die out here. Why didn't you just leave us in Egypt, Moses? At least we had water there!" All of a sudden Moses was surrounded by angry people, fists shaking in the air. "Wa-ter, Wa-ter!" they chanted.

"God, HELP ME! These people are getting angrier by the minute," Moses quickly prayed. "What am I going to do? There isn't any water around here. But, if you don't do something, they're going to stone me to death!" God answered right away, "Take some of the leaders and go to Mt. Sinai. I'll meet you by a big rock there."

Quickly Moses called the leaders together and they left the shouting mob behind. "Moses, this is the rock," God said. "Hit it with your shepherd's staff." Moses could hear the angry people behind him as he lifted his staff and slammed it down on the rock. Just as it cracked against the stone, water gushed from the rock. Everyone drank all they wanted. Once again, God had taken care of his people . . . and helped Moses.

Based on Exodus 17:1-6

Becoming a Man of God
A man of God sees God's power

How many times were the Israelites going to complain about the way things were going for them? When Moses first told them that God had called him to lead them out of Egypt, he did a miracle to prove God was with him. Then, God sent ten terrible plagues on the Egyptians to convince Pharaoh to let the people go. Next, God parted the waters of the Red Sea to save them from the Egyptian army. But, the Israelites must have had very short memories, because at the slightest little problem, they started complaining and shouting at Moses again. That must have made God very sad.

But, every time the Israelites complained, Moses turned to God and asked, "What do I do now?" Each time, God answered Moses' problem with a wonderful miracle. Imagine the people's surprise when Moses smacked the rock with his shepherd's staff and water poured out. God is really awesome, isn't he?

Think about examples of God's power that you have seen. If you haven't seen a "miracle" then think about the everyday displays of his power, in weather or in the sun coming up every day. What are some other God-power-shows?

Dad's Turn

Have you ever been on a camping trip where you were hot and tired and thirsty? Tell your son about the experience. Did you ever get frustrated with the leaders because of your discomfort?

When have you been most impressed with God's power? Have you been obviously aware of God's power in your life? Tell your son about it; share with him how God's power is evident and important in your life.

Talk with your son about God's power. Talk about how God's power so often takes care of us. Some things we take for granted that keep us safe every day—warmth from the sun, gravity to keep us in place, air to breathe. Talk about awesome displays of God's power, such as lightning storms, volcanoes, tornadoes, and gentle displays of his power, such as beautiful sunsets or the creation of something as delicate as a butterfly.

A Verse to Remember

Power, O God, belongs to you.

Psalm 62:11

Yellow-Bellied Chickens!

"**Y**ou've dragged us all over this wilderness in search of the Promised Land," a man complained to Moses. "We're tired of searching; we want to see it."

"Funny you should say that," Moses smiled, "because we're here. We're right outside the Promised Land. God wants you to see how great it is, so I'm sending in twelve spies to see what the land is like and how well the cities are protected. Then, we'll know what we're getting into before we attack."

A few days later the twelve spies were sneaking into the country, sliding down mountains, crossing over rivers, seeing what the land was like. "Wow! Look at the size of those grapes over there!" one spy called. "Let's take some back to show Moses and the rest of the people. This land is incredible!" Everywhere the men searched, the land looked great . . . except for the really, really big people who lived there.

"We're back!" Forty days after sneaking into the Promised Land, the spies returned to Moses and the Israelites, carrying the giant grapes on their shoulders. "The land is awesome. It's like nothing you've seen before . . . good crops, good water . . . but . . ."

"When you say 'but' that means something bad! What is it?" someone called out.

"Well, there is this one little problem of the giant people who live there and the big walls around every city," one spy mumbled.

"Never mind that!" Joshua and Caleb shouted. "God said that the land is ours. All we have to do is trust him . . . and go for it!"

"Don't be crazy!" the other ten spies cried out, with their chicken hearts on their sleeves. "There's no way we could beat those giants!" The people listened as the ten spies argued with the two spies.

Finally they said, "Majority rules. There's no way we're going to try to capture the land!"

Caleb and Joshua were so frustrated that they wanted to stomp on all the giant grapes. "Why couldn't the people just trust God?"

God was even more frustrated than they were. "I told you I was giving you the land. Since you don't believe me, you can just wander around in the desert for forty years. Then, I'll give the land to your children. All of you, except Caleb and Joshua, will be dead. They are the only two who can see the Promised Land."

Based on Numbers 13-14

Becoming a Man of God
A man of God trusts God

What was it going to take to get the Israelites to actually trust God? He already told them that he was giving them the land of Canaan, but only Moses, Joshua, and Caleb believed him. The rest of the spies and all the people were yellow-bellied chickens!

Of course, trust isn't easy because it means believing someone will (or can) do what they say they will do . . . even when you can't actually see anything happening. Trust is hard the first time you trust someone, but, the Israelites had certainly seen God's power before this. They should have been able to trust him to give them the land of Canaan.

Have you ever trusted someone to do something, then been disappointed because they didn't come through? How did you feel? Have you ever trusted someone to keep a promise and they did? How did you feel then?

Dad's Turn

Are you a trusting person? Do you trust people to keep their word or follow through on what they tell you? Tell your son about a time when someone made a promise to you and did follow through on it. How did you feel? Remind him of a promise you once made to him that you kept. Ask him if that made him more willing to trust you the next time.

Remind your son of the many promises God gives us in his Word—his promise to forgive our sins, to love us, to help us with our problems. Share with him that the stories in the Bible are examples of the way God keeps his word . . . so we know we can trust him! Trusting God gives great peace and comfort that he will answer prayers and keep the promises he has already given in his Word.

A Verse to Remember

The LORD your God is indeed God.
He is the faithful God who keeps
his covenant for a thousand generations
and constantly loves those
who love him and obey his commands.

Deuteronomy 7:9

Whiners and Complainers

"Where are you taking us now? Are we ever going to stop walking around this desert?" Everywhere Moses turned someone was whining and complaining. "Why did you bring us out of Egypt anyway?" "Yeah," someone else jumped in, "it wasn't so bad being slaves . . . at least we had food and water!"

"Yeah . . . real food! I'm sick of this manna stuff."

"Aarrghh." Moses was so frustrated. "You wouldn't even have manna if it wasn't for God. He sends you that food from heaven every day."

"But day in and day out it's manna, manna, manna. I remember fresh fruit and meat. We used to have something different every day!" another man shouted.

God heard the people complaining about the very miracles he was doing to take care of them. He knew that he had to do something to get their attention again. The people walked down into a small valley, still complaining and whining, and suddenly there were snakes everywhere, even in the trees and high up on the rocks. They couldn't get away from the snakes.

"Aaaahhh, that snake bit me! Help me, I'm going to die!"
People everywhere were screaming and crying for help.
"Moses, pray that God will take the snakes away. Please,
we're sorry for complaining so much. Ask him to help us!"
Just as he had so many times already, Moses asked God to
help the people.

"Make a fake snake that looks just like these snakes and put it on a tall pole. The people simply have to look at it and their snakebites will be healed," God said. Moses made a snake out of bronze and told the people to look at it.

"Just looking at a bronze snake will heal us?" The people were amazed. But, everyone who obeyed the command was healed. Once again God saved his people.

Based on Numbers 21:4-9

Becoming a Man of God
A man of God doesn't complain

Those Israelites complained about everything, didn't they? Every time Moses turned around they had some new complaint. God was sending them food from heaven every single day, and they complained that they had to eat the same thing every day.

Moses, on the other hand, was better at looking at the blessings God was giving them every day and being thankful for God's love and care. Like the old saying, Moses looked at the glass of water and saw it as half full, but the Israelites saw it as half empty.

Do you complain about stuff? Come on, be honest. A good clue would be if you've heard your parents tell you to stop whining. What kinds of things do you complain about? Is it usually because you want your way about something, or because someone doesn't do what you want exactly when you want them to?

Dad's Turn

All of us are guilty of complaining at some time. Tell your son about a time when you complained. Why were you unhappy with the situation? Were you later sorry for complaining? How did the people around you handle your attitude?

Point out that, even though the Israelites were complaining again, God once again met their need. He did another miracle to save them—but they had a part in this miracle. They had to actually look at the bronze snake in order to be healed from a snakebite. So, while God did do a miracle, the people had to believe that he was offering a way to save them. Again and again God sent the message, "Trust me!"

Does your son have a habit of complaining? Talk to him about it now. Help him begin to see that complaining is a selfish habit. Talk to him about learning to be patient and wait for his requests to be answered. Talk about trusting God to answer his prayers. Sometimes it takes lots of patience and trust to wait on God for his timing in answering our prayers—and we shouldn't be complaining in the meantime.

A Verse to Remember

The Lord is wonderfully good to those
who wait for him and seek him.

Lamentations 3:25

The Donkey and the Angel

"King Balak wants to see me. ME!" Balaam was pretty excited.

But God said, "Don't go to Balak. He wants you to hurt my people."

Even so, early the next morning Balaam climbed on his donkey and headed out to see the king. God was not happy with him.

God doesn't want him to go...

Balaam hummed a tune as he rode along. *Balak promised me lots of money for my help and I can think of lots of ways to spend it,* he thought. But, suddenly Balaam's donkey bolted off the road and into a field. "What are you doing?" Balaam shouted, hitting the donkey with a stick and pulling it back to the road.

What was that all about? Balaam wondered. "OWWW," he
screamed as the donkey slammed his leg into a wall. "There's
plenty of room between these buildings. Why are you
smashing me into the wall?" Balaam beat the donkey again.

A few minutes later the donkey laid down in the middle of the road, and nothing Balaam did would make him get up. Balaam raised his arm to beat the donkey again, but his arm stopped in midair when the donkey said, "Why are you hitting me? I'm just trying to protect you."

"Did you just . . . speak?" Balaam was pretty confused—who ever heard of a talking donkey? Just then God let Balaam see what the donkey had been seeing all along . . . an angel in the middle of the road holding a sword high in the air. "Oh wow! I was disobeying God by going to see the king. You saved me from God's anger!" Balaam realized. Now Balaam was thankful for his donkey's stubbornness.

Based on Numbers 22:21-34

Becoming a Man of God

A man of God keeps his priorities straight

Balaam got his priorities messed up. Do you wonder what that means? Balaam knew in his heart that the most important thing was to obey God. But, when King Balak offered him lots of money to do what he wanted, Balaam forgot about obeying God. He got dollar signs in his eyes!

God got his attention in a pretty cool way, didn't he? A talking donkey! Wow! God gave Balaam a second chance to obey him, by letting the donkey see the angel in the road and doing what it could to stop Balaam from going to the king.

What do you think should be the most important thing for you to do? Obey God? Obey your parents? Is it ever hard for you to do that because your friends or brothers or sisters try to get you to disobey? Or is it ever hard because something you want to do looks so appealing . . . even though it would be disobeying to do it?

Dad's Turn

It may not be easy for you to admit to your son that you sometimes get your priorities mixed up. But, more than likely you have at one time or another. Tell your son about it. Perhaps you once got so caught up in your career that your relationship with your family was sacrificed. Maybe it became more important to make money than to spend time with God. Tell your son how you came to realize your priorities were wrong. What did you do once you made that realization?

Make a list together of things that are important to you and your son. Now, prioritize that list. Talk about how to keep things in perspective and keep the thing in first place that should be there.

A Verse to Remember

Seek his will in all you do,
and he will direct your paths.

Proverbs 3:6

Million-Man March

God never forgets. He promised to give the Israelites their own land and even though it had been a long time, he hadn't forgotten that promise. Joshua was the Israelites' leader, since Moses died. "God wants us to set up camp outside the city of Jericho," he announced to his people.

"That city is locked up tight and has big walls around it," one man said.

"That's OK. God says that Jericho will be ours. We must trust him and do exactly what he tells us to do," Joshua answered.

"All right!" the people shouted, high-fiving each other and celebrating. "Those Jericho-ites won't even know what hit them!" "Yeah, we're going to do some serious city-capturing!"

"Hold on." Joshua stopped the celebration. "We're going to do exactly what God says. He wants us to march around the city once a day for six days—and not say a word!"

"What? The men of Jericho will think we're crazy!" "Yeah, we'll look like fools!" the people complained. But, Joshua wouldn't budge. "It's God's way or no way!"

"HA! Look at those crazy Israelites!" the men of Jericho laughed. "What are they trying to do, shake the walls and make them fall down?"

Once a day for six days the Israelites silently marched around the city, then went back to their camp. By the sixth day, the men of Jericho were making so much fun of them that the Israelites wondered if Joshua really knew what he was doing.

The seventh day the people of Jericho woke up to the sound of the Israelites marching again. "Why don't they go away?" people moaned as they rolled over and went back to sleep. Some people did notice that the Israelites didn't stop after one time around. *Ahh, it's just some new wrinkle in their silly plan,* they thought. Six times Joshua led the people around the city. By then, crowds of people were on the walls making fun of the army and throwing water and other stuff at them. But, even with water dripping in his eyes, Joshua kept marching.

"Hey, fools, you're gonna wear out your shoes with all that marching!" the men of Jericho called.

When the Israelites started their seventh time around the city, Joshua called, "Shout, the Lord has given you this city!" The Israelites gave out a loud, "Whoop!" and the priests blared on their horns. The men standing on the big walls fell off as the walls crumbled and fell. The Israelites raced in and captured Jericho. God gave them the city, just as he said.

Based on Joshua 6

Becoming a Man of God
A man of God does exactly what God says

The Israelites seem to be learning to trust . . . trust their leader and trust God. When they heard that God was giving them the city of Jericho, they were ready to take it by storm. They even wanted to gloat a little bit . . . kind of rub it in to the men of Jericho that they were going to capture that city, no matter what! They wanted to have a real show of power. But, God had other ideas. He wanted the people to know that Jericho was being captured by his power—not theirs.

So, when Joshua laid down the law—it's God's way or no way—the Israelites agreed. Don't you imagine that they felt silly marching around the city walls every day for six days, not saying a word, not shooting an arrow, not doing anything but marching? But, God was true to his word. The city was theirs, and there was no doubt that it was because of God's power!

How good are you at following instructions? Do you find it hard to exactly follow what you are told to do? When was a time that you didn't follow instructions and later were sorry? When was a time that you did follow instructions exactly and were glad?

Dad's Turn

Dad, do you read the instructions before you assemble a piece of furniture, or before using a new appliance? Is reading the instructions a last resort for you? Tell your son about a time when your neglect to follow instructions caused a problem. What happened? Did it cause you extra work to correct the situation? Were you sorry that you didn't follow instructions?

Remind your son of a time when he followed instructions you gave him. Tell him how pleased you were with his attention to detail and obedience. Tell him how proud you were of him.

God is pleased with us when we follow instructions he gives us. His instructions are given in the Bible. One good place to look is the Ten Commandments—good instructions for how to live for him and how to treat other people. It's important to exactly follow his instructions, and not try to reword them to fit the way we live.

A Verse to Remember

Teach me to do your will,
for you are my God.

Psalm 143:10

The Longest Day

Spears soared through the air and swords clashed! Joshua's army won another battle. His army of Israelites destroyed or captured every enemy they fought against. The king of Gibeon heard about Joshua's victories . . . and offered to be friends. "It's better to fight with them than against them!" he told his soldiers.

"Hey, if we're going to stand any chance against Joshua's army, we've got to forget our differences and fight together as one army." Adoni-zedek, the king of Jerusalem, explained his plan to four other Amorite kings. "Let's attack Gibeon and capture their army. That will bring Joshua's army down to a normal size."

When the Amorites attacked, the king of Gibeon sent a
message to Joshua asking for help. "Come on, men. We've
got to help our friends!" Joshua and the Israelites traveled
all night to Gibeon. Their early morning attack surprised the
Amorites and the battle began!

"Let's get out of here. We can't beat these guys!" The Amorites took off running, but as they ran . . . "OW, now it's hailing huge hailstones. What else can go wrong?" The Amorites knew they were never going to beat Joshua's army. God sent the biggest, hardest hailstones ever. More soldiers were killed by hailstones than in the battle.

"Wow, it feels like we've been fighting for hours. But, the sun hasn't even moved, so it can't have been that long," one Israelite soldier said, dropping to the ground for a rest.

"No, it has been a long time. Before the battle, Joshua asked God to make the sun and moon stand still until we won—and God did!"

(Never before that time, and never since has God made the sun and moon stand still!)

Based on Joshua 10:1-15

Becoming a Man of God

A man of God isn't afraid to ask for a miracle

Joshua really wanted to win this battle. He knew that his army was the army of God, and he didn't want God's enemies to defeat him. He also knew that if the battle wasn't won by sundown, it would stop for the day because they couldn't fight in the dark. It might pick up the next day, or it might just be considered a tie and never be continued. Joshua really wanted to WIN!

So, he asked God to do a miracle. He asked him to keep daylight shining until the battle was won . . . and God did! Joshua believed that God has that kind of power and that he is willing to share that power with his people, if we ask him to.

Have you ever asked God to do a miracle? Did you believe in your heart that he could do it, and that he would? What was your request? What happened?

Dad's Turn

If you have a true story of a miracle God did in response
to your prayer, tell your son about it. When was a time
when you sincerely prayed for God to do a miracle? What
happened? We often pray for God to supernaturally heal
a loved one, or show his power in some supernatural way,
as he did for Joshua. In our world today, miracles are often
explained away or denied. Help your son understand that the
God of the Old Testament can still do miracles in our world, if
he chooses to do so. But, remind your son that if God doesn't
answer his prayers with a miracle, it doesn't mean he isn't
listening. It only means that the miracle wasn't in his plans.

Look at some situations you have prayed for and see if
you can pick out small answers to prayer, even if God didn't
send the "big miracle" you asked for.

A Verse to Remember

We can be confident
that he will listen to us
whenever we ask him for anything
in line with his will.

1 John 5:14

Battle Plan!

"Send out the word! Every able-bodied man must join the army! We're going to beat those Midianites once and for all!" Gideon was determined to have the biggest army Israel had ever seen! Soon more than 30,000 men were ready to fight.

"Uh-uh," God said. "If you win with that many soldiers, the Israelites will think they won without my help. Some of the soldiers have to go."

"OK," Gideon agreed. "Anyone who is scared can go home!" he shouted. Twenty thousand men left.

"Take your 10,000 men down to the river and tell them to get a drink," God said. While the men drank, Gideon walked around watching them.

"What's he looking at?" one soldier whispered. "I don't know, but I feel weird with him watching every move I make," another answered.

Suddenly Gideon shouted, "Every man who scooped water up in his hands must stay! Everyone else can go home!" Now Gideon's army was down to 300 soldiers.

"We're going to whip those Midianites!" Gideon promised. "I know there are thousands more of them than there are of us. But, God is fighting on our side! Count off by threes, and go stand with your group. This is how we're going to win . . ." Gideon told the soldiers the plan that God had given him.

Around midnight the soldiers sneaked up on the Midianites. Each one carried a horn and a torch covered with a clay jar. One soldier bumped his jar against something and the "ping" rang out in the darkness. "Shh! We gotta be quiet until Gideon gives us the sign." Just then Gideon shouted and according to the battle plan, they broke the jars. The glowing torches and tooting horns scared the Midianites. They ran all over each other in their hurry to get away. Gideon's little army won!

Based on Judges 7

Becoming a Man of God
A man of God trusts God's power

Gideon had a good plan . . . get the biggest army together he could, then attack the enemy and beat them soundly!

But, God had a different plan. He wanted everyone to know that this battle would be won by his power, not because Gideon had a big army. Imagine how the soldiers who remained felt as Gideon kept sending other soldiers home. They saw their army dwindle down to 300 men from 30,000. Do you think they were scared? Do you think they felt like they didn't have a chance against the big Midianite army? When God decides to do something, it will happen, however he chooses.

The whole foundation of life with God is that you must trust him. Trust his word, his power, and his love. Think about a time when you've seen God's power displayed. How did it make you feel?

Dad's Turn

"Trust God" . . . easy words to say, aren't they? But, sometimes they aren't so easy to live out. Can you recall a time from your childhood when you needed and found God's power? How about when your family moved to a new town and you really needed some new friends? Did you pray about it? Then, all of a sudden a week or so later, did you realize that God had given you new friends? Was that coincidence, or a display of God's power in the hearts of your new friends?

In our world, we tend to think that bigger is better. Can you and your son think of some examples of times when bigger is not better? Why is it important to know that things happen because of God's power and not because of ours? When you know that God's power is working, does that make it easier to trust him the next time?

A Verse to Remember

So be strong and take courage,
all you who put your hope in the LORD!

Psalm 31:24

A Voice in the Darkness

Samuel always said his prayers before bedtime: "God bless Momma and keep her safe. God bless Mr. Eli and take care of him . . . and God bless me and help me learn everything I can to be your servant. Amen." Little Samuel lived in the temple with the priest, Eli, because his momma had promised God that if he gave her a son, she would give him back to serve God. So, Samuel learned everything Eli taught him. He was a good boy and he took his work very seriously.

After one especially long day of temple work, Samuel was snoozing away, when something interrupted his sleep. He rolled over and rubbed his eyes awake. "Samuel, Samuel." Someone was calling his name. Climbing out of bed and sliding into his slippers he ran to Eli's room. "Yes, Sir, what do you want?"

The funny thing was, Eli was still snoring away. He hadn't called Samuel! "Go back to bed," Eli mumbled.

That was weird, Samuel thought as he climbed under the blankets once again. He was just dozing off when he heard, "Samuel, Samuel." Jumping out of bed, he dashed to Eli's room, knocking his knee on the door frame. "Owww," he moaned. "Eli, what do you want?" he asked with a little impatience creeping into his voice.

"Why do you keep waking me up? I didn't call you. Go back to bed!" Eli sounded a little impatient, too.

That was weirder than ever, Samuel thought. *Am I dreaming this or what?* He sat on the edge of his bed for awhile trying to figure out what was going on. Finally, he got so sleepy that he fell over on the pillow. A gentle voice woke him up. "Samuel, Samuel."

"This isn't funny!" he announced, stomping into Eli's room. "Yes?" he asked, a bit loudly. Now the old priest knew what was going on. He told Samuel exactly what to do when he heard the voice again.

Samuel got back into bed, but he didn't go to sleep. He lay very still, waiting for the voice to speak again. Sure enough, he heard, "Samuel, Samuel."

"Yes, Lord, I'm listening," he answered, just as Eli had told him to do. *Eli was right, the voice is from God. I wonder what God wants to say to me*, Samuel wondered. He listened very carefully to everything God said. That night Samuel learned an important lesson about listening when God calls.

Based on 1 Samuel 3

Becoming a Man of God
A man of God listens for God's voice

Samuel was just a little boy who heard God call his name. That might be something you would expect to happen to an adult, but not a child. What would God want with a child? Why would he choose to speak to a child instead of an adult? Well, God looks at a person's heart to see if they truly love and care about him. He saw that Samuel did, so he trusted Samuel with an important message.

It is important to know that Samuel would not have heard God's message if he hadn't been quiet so he could hear God's voice. Also, when Eli told him what to do to hear God's message, Samuel did it.

Have you ever dreamed something that seemed so real that you were sure it had actually happened? Maybe that's how Samuel felt. Samuel found out that it was God's voice speaking to him because he was quiet and listened for him.

Dad's Turn

How good are you at listening? When your son talks to you, do you listen with full attention? Do you really hear what he says or do you partially listen to him while you are doing something else at the same time?

Tell your son about a time when you only partially listened to instructions or news and later were sorry that you didn't have all the information.

Talk to your son about spending time in silence, where you can hear God speak to you. Together read a verse of Scripture, then just be quiet together while you each think about what it means.

A Verse to Remember

Be silent and know that I am God.

Psalm 46:10

Wisdom and Love

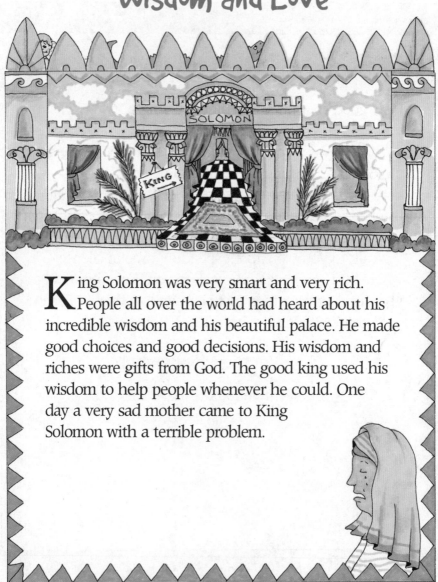

King Solomon was very smart and very rich. People all over the world had heard about his incredible wisdom and his beautiful palace. He made good choices and good decisions. His wisdom and riches were gifts from God. The good king used his wisdom to help people whenever he could. One day a very sad mother came to King Solomon with a terrible problem.

"O great King, please help me," the woman said. She pointed to another woman who was holding a small baby. "That woman stole my baby," she whispered.

"Did not!" the woman said, hugging the baby tightly.

"We both had babies," the first woman continued. "During the night her baby died. So, she took my live baby and put her dead child beside me."

"NO!" screamed the second woman. "She's lying! She's trying to steal my baby!"

The great and wise king looked at both women and thought for a few moments about how to handle the situation. Both women jumped when he loudly commanded, "Bring a sword. Cut this child in two and give half to each woman!" For a few seconds it seemed that no one in the room even breathed.

"NO!" the first woman screamed. "Don't hurt him; please don't hurt the baby! Let her keep him." She fell to the floor, sobbing and crying.

Everyone was amazed, when, at the very same time, the second woman held the baby out to the guard. "Fine!" she shouted. "Kill him. If I can't have him, then neither can she!"

King Solomon smiled calmly. "Stop," he commanded. "Give the child to the first woman. She is the true mother."

She looked up at the king in amazement. "How do you know that for sure?" she whispered through her tears.

King Solomon took her hand and pulled her to her feet. "Because the real mother would rather give up her child than let him be hurt," he said. The woman hugged her child, knowing deep in her heart that the king's great wisdom was truly a gift from God.

Based on 1 Kings 3:16-28

Becoming a Man of God
A man of God helps others

King Solomon's wisdom was a gift from God. He treasured this gift and used it to help other people, not just for his own benefit. He knew that the child's real mother would do pretty much anything to save her child and keep him safe. He also knew that the other woman wouldn't care if the child was killed.

God gives each of his children different gifts and talents. It must make him happy when we use those gifts and talents to help others. The more we help one another the better life is for all of us.

How do you help other people? What are some things you could do for your family or neighbors, even as a child? How do others help you? What do your family members do for you?

Dad's Turn

If your son sees you helping people whenever you can, he will learn to do the same thing. Tell him about a time when you went out of your way to help someone. How did the other person feel? How did you feel? Tell him about a time when someone helped you. How did you feel? What are the skills or talents you have that you willingly share with others?

Talk with your son about ways he can help other people. What are some practical things he can do for the family or for elderly neighbors? How can you and your son increase your level of wisdom? Talk about topics you both would like to know more about. Can you read books or watch videos about these topics? Decide on a plan for increasing your knowledge of God and his Word. Are there other books besides this one that can help you know God better?

A Verse to Remember

Two people can accomplish more than
twice as much as one;
they get a better return for their labor.
If one person falls,
the other can reach out and help.
But people who are alone when they fall
are in real trouble.

Ecclesiastes 4:9-10

A Very Important Baby

Joseph always tried to do the right thing. So, when the angel told him that Mary was going to have a baby boy who was the Son of God, Joseph not only believed the angel—he went ahead with his plans to marry her. "I promise you, God, that I will be a good earthly father to your Son. I'll take good care of him!" he prayed.

Just before it was time for the baby to be born, everyone in the kingdom was ordered to go to the city where their families were from. The ruler wanted to count how many people lived in his kingdom!

"Ohhh, this baby is trying to kick his way into the world. Are we almost there?" Mary moaned.

"Yes, we'll soon be in Bethlehem and we'll get a nice room in the inn." Joseph felt bad for Mary. The baby in her tummy kicked harder with every step the donkey took. She could have stayed in Nazareth while he went for the census, but it was so close to time for the baby to be born that she didn't want to be away from him.

When they finally reached the crowded streets of Bethlehem, the town was filled with people who had come for the census. "I don't feel so good," Mary whispered, holding her hand over her mouth.

"It is pretty smelly," Joseph admitted. The scent of sweaty bodies and dirty animals even made his stomach turn a bit. "Just sit tight and I'll get us a room. Then you can rest on a soft bed." But, in only a few minutes Joseph was back with bad news. "The inn is full. There's not a room available in the whole town!"

"The innkeeper said we can stay in his stable, if we want. Mary, I'm so sorry!" Joseph felt terrible.

"It will be OK. I just want to get off this donkey," Mary moaned. In the stable Joseph pulled clean hay from the loft and made a bed for Mary, who quickly fell asleep. He was feeding the donkey when Mary cried, "The baby is coming! Oh, please, not in a stable. Joseph, do something!" But there was nothing to do, except hold her hand until the baby was born. Joseph watched in awe as Mary wrapped Jesus in strips of cloth.

"Mary, you must be exhausted," Joseph whispered. He reached to touch the baby's hand, but just then some shepherds peeked into the stable.

"An angel came to us tonight, well—hundreds of angels. They told us that this baby is the Son of God, the Messiah," one shepherd said. "They said that this baby will save his people from their sins."

Joseph looked at the baby again and remembered when the angel told him that Mary's baby was the Son of God. *It's true*, he thought, *this child is the Messiah.*

Based on Matthew 1:20-25; Luke 2:1-20

Becoming a Man of God
A man of God recognizes his Messiah

Joseph must have loved God and tried his best to obey him. After all, God's angel encouraged Joseph to marry young Mary and that meant he would be Jesus' earthly father. Joseph obeyed the angel and went ahead with the marriage plans. Maybe he didn't fully understand what it meant that the baby was God's Son. But, when the shepherds announced that hundreds of angels had spoken to them, Joseph must have known for sure that this baby was someone special!

Joseph took the responsibility of caring for Jesus very seriously. But, imagine how he felt when he looked at the newborn baby and understood that he was responsible for providing for and caring for the Messiah—the Savior that the Jewish people had been waiting hundreds of years for.

Do you believe that Jesus is your Savior? Do you understand that the little baby whose birth we celebrate at Christmas grew up to die on a cross for your sins? Then, God brought him back to life and now he is back in heaven with God.

Dad's Turn

Tell your son a favorite childhood Christmas memory—a family tradition or a trip to Grandma's house, or perhaps a program that you were part of. Tell him if your family was normally part of some holiday ministry, such as providing gifts for inner city kids. If your family isn't currently sharing in a holiday ministry, talk about something you could get involved in.

Share with your son the story of your own salvation. Tell him how you came to realize that Jesus is your Savior. How old were you? Who explained the plan of salvation to you?

Has your son made a decision for Christ? If not, talk to him about it now. Make sure he understands the plan of salvation.

A Verse to Remember

For God so loved the world that
he gave his only Son,
so that everyone who believes in him
will not perish but have eternal life.

John 3:16

Starlight!

Amazingly, Jesus was pretty much like any other two-year-old. He liked to play with his toys. He liked to catch the soap bubbles Mary blew at him while she did laundry. The little family stayed in Bethlehem after the baby was born. Joseph set up a carpentry business and kept pretty busy, even if his kind heart sometimes made him charge less than his products were worth. Mary was happy, but sometimes she missed her mom. She wished her family could see Jesus grow up . . . and give her advice about how to be a mother.

Mary blew a bubble toward Jesus and thought about what the angel had told her and Joseph before the little guy was born. She remembered the shepherds peeking into the stable, whispering, "The Messiah. The Messiah is born." She wondered what it all meant. *I wonder what's ahead for this little guy?*

Mary and Joseph had made friends in Bethlehem. While Joseph worked away in his carpenter shop, Mary and other young mothers did their household chores. Sometimes they stopped to chat with each other and let their children play together. But, Joseph and Mary never mentioned anything to anyone about who Jesus really was.

One morning Mary heard a commotion outside. "Who are those expensive gifts for?" the neighbors whispered back and forth. Standing in the front yard were the fanciest-looking men Mary had ever seen. Soon the entire town had gathered to see what the men were going to do. "We have come from very far away to worship the child who is the king of the Jews," the strangers announced.

Well, that should make the neighbors curious, thought Mary.

"How did you find us?" she asked. One of the men pointed to the star that was hovering right over their house. "We've been following that star for the last two years. It moved across the sky, but it stopped when it got to your house," he said. "We brought gifts for the little king."

The strangers laid gifts of gold, frankincense, and myrhh in front of little Jesus. Amazingly, he seemed to understand what was happening. He didn't make a peep or move a bit. "Thank you, dear God. Thank you for this precious child," Mary's heart whispered.

Based on Matthew 2:1-12

Becoming a Man of God
A man of God gives gifts to the King

The wise men traveled a long, long way to find young Jesus. They brought him very special gifts because they wanted to give him the best they had to give. They knew that's what he deserved. They wanted to honor the young boy who was the Savior of the world. They must have had a strong belief in and respect for God. They also honored Jesus by going home a different way instead of telling King Herod where they had found the young boy.

What gifts can you bring to Jesus? You probably don't have lots of money. You can't go anywhere without your mom or dad taking you . . . so what can you give? Is he important enough to you that you want to give him gifts . . . your best gifts? List some things that you can give Jesus right now.

Dad's Turn

What is the absolute best gift you have ever received? Was it Christmas, birthday, or some other time? What made it so special? Who gave it to you? Do you still have it?

What is the best gift you've ever given to someone? Were you excited to give it? Who was it for? Why was it special?

Tell your son some of the ways you give gifts to God. Don't forget the time you give to his work at church or Sunday school. Remember everyday things like cutting an elderly neighbor's lawn, or special times when you have volunteered at a homeless shelter. Help your son see that there are many ways to give gifts to God, and not all of them involve money. He wants our hearts to love him and love other people. We can serve in that way.

Help your son complete his list of ways he can serve God. Can you think of some things you can do together?

A Verse to Remember

[God] will not forget how hard you have worked
for him and how you have shown your love
to him by caring for other Christians.

Hebrews 6:10

Bug and Honey Sandwiches

"Stop doing bad things! Turn to God!" a loud voice shouted. People walking along the road or working in the nearby fields stopped and looked around.

"Did you hear something?" they asked each other. A few minutes later the voice rang out again, "Why are you just pretending to know God? Do you really think that you're fooling him?"

When the man who belonged to the voice stepped out into the light, a rumble of questions rolled through the crowd. "What is that he is wearing?" "It looks like . . . camel skin." "Whew! I bet he hasn't had a bath in weeks!" "Do you think he has ever cut his hair?" John ignored the whispered comments and went right on preaching.

"Why are you yelling at us? We don't need to worry about this stuff. Our great-great-granddaddy was Abraham, a famous man of God . . . or is it great-great-great-granddaddy? I forget. Anyway, we come from a good line. We're all set with God, so go on and do your preaching somewhere else." The man gave John a little shove that sent him on down the road.

431

"Wait a minute," another man said. "I've heard of you. You're John the Baptist. You live out in the wilderness by yourself. Your clothes are made of camel skins and you eat bugs and honey. [When he said that, some of the women got sick to their stomachs.] Some people say that you're the one the prophet Isaiah wrote about. They say that you're getting people ready to meet the Messiah." By this time a big crowd was gathered around John.

"Yes, I baptize people with water, which shows that they are turning away from their sins. But, the Messiah is coming soon and he will baptize people with the Holy Spirit. He will separate good people from bad people. He knows the difference. Be ready!" With that, John walked away, preaching his message of warning to any and all who would listen.

Based on Luke 3:1-20

Becoming a Man of God
A man of God tells about Jesus

Way back before John the Baptist was even born, an angel told his parents that his job would be to tell people that Jesus was coming. He spent his life telling people that Jesus, the Savior, was coming. When people believed his message, he baptized them in a river to show that they were turning away from their sins and deciding to live for God. John knew what his job was and he gave his life to that work. He knew that people were sinners and he told them so—right to their faces.

How can you tell people about Jesus? Do you have to wear camel-skin clothes and eat bugs to be Jesus' worker? Of course not; the way you live your life and the way you treat people every day shows them what God's love is like. You also can invite friends to come to church, Sunday school, or special programs with you where they can hear that God loves them.

Dad's Turn

John the Baptist didn't pull any punches. People were sinning and he told them so. Christians continue to do that today by being different—not weird but different—in our approach and attitudes to situations that life presents.

After reading the story of John the Baptist, explain to your son how all members of God's family work together to share the news of God's love with the world. Some people are good at preaching, some are good at music, some are good at being friends or helping out people with problems. Share with your son the way you feel God uses you to tell people about him. For example, you may be a good mechanic, so your personal ministry is that of fixing cars and showing people Christian love in action.

Help your son see ways that he can share God's love with his friends. Explain to him how he can stand up for what is right when others are doing something wrong. Help him to realize the ways he shares God's love. Reinforce his kind treatment of others and his sensitive heart.

A Verse to Remember

You are the light of the world—
like a city on a mountain,
glowing in the night for all to see.

Matthew 5:14

A Happy Ending

"O God, please help my son get well. I know you gave him to me and he is so special to me. He's been sick a long time and no matter what I do he just seems to get worse. Please, God, since my husband died, this boy is all the family I have." The worried mother rocked her son, put cool rags on his feverish forehead, and prayed for all she was worth.

Even though the mother did everything she could think of, the boy died. With her heart aching, the woman sat beside her dead son's bed, holding his limp hand. She remembered how he used to run and laugh and play with his friends.

Friends brought food and flowers to her, but the sad momma didn't seem to notice. She just sat and stared at her son's body. Finally, her friends began making funeral arrangements. They thought the woman would sit beside her dead son forever if they didn't take charge.

On the day of the funeral one of her friends actually took the woman's hand and led her out of the house. Other friends lifted the boy's coffin to their shoulders, and family and friends followed along behind them to go bury the boy. The sad little parade walked through town as people on the street and in the shops watched them pass, feeling sorry for the sad mother.

At the city gate, the funeral procession had to wait while people came into town. A group of men stepped aside to let the funeral pass. *It isn't hard to tell who the mother of the dead boy is*, the men thought. Her body was so filled with grief that she could barely walk. Suddenly one of the men stepped up to the woman and took her hand. "Don't be sad," he said softly. The people who heard thought he was crazy. How could he say that when she had just lost her only son?

His words made sense when the man stepped up to the coffin and took the dead boy's hand. "Get up," he said. To everyone's amazement, the dead boy sat up! "Who is that guy?" people began asking each other.

"It's Jesus, the teacher from Nazareth," someone said. Jesus took the woman's hand and gently placed the boy's hand in it. He smiled at the joy in her face and laughed out loud when she pulled her alive-again-son into her arms, hugging him for all she was worth.

Based on Luke 7:11-17

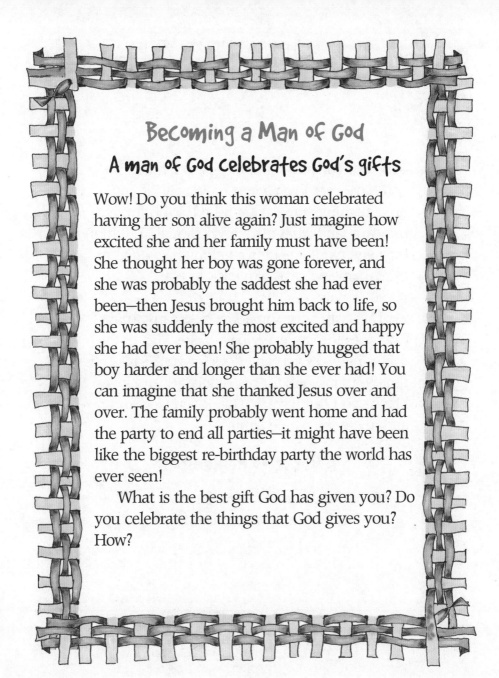

Becoming a Man of God
A man of God celebrates God's gifts

Wow! Do you think this woman celebrated having her son alive again? Just imagine how excited she and her family must have been! She thought her boy was gone forever, and she was probably the saddest she had ever been–then Jesus brought him back to life, so she was suddenly the most excited and happy she had ever been! She probably hugged that boy harder and longer than she ever had! You can imagine that she thanked Jesus over and over. The family probably went home and had the party to end all parties–it might have been like the biggest re-birthday party the world has ever seen!

What is the best gift God has given you? Do you celebrate the things that God gives you? How?

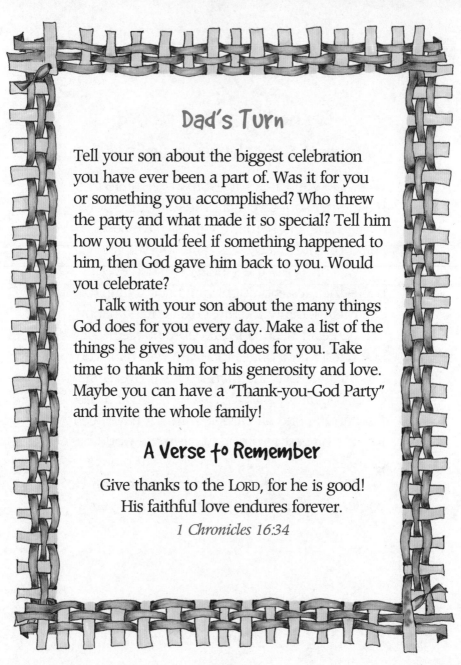

Dad's Turn

Tell your son about the biggest celebration you have ever been a part of. Was it for you or something you accomplished? Who threw the party and what made it so special? Tell him how you would feel if something happened to him, then God gave him back to you. Would you celebrate?

Talk with your son about the many things God does for you every day. Make a list of the things he gives you and does for you. Take time to thank him for his generosity and love. Maybe you can have a "Thank-you-God Party" and invite the whole family!

A Verse to Remember

Give thanks to the LORD, for he is good!
His faithful love endures forever.

1 Chronicles 16:34

The Master's Money

"Hey you, the master wants to see you." The foreman tapped a servant on the back. "You, too . . . and you over there." He singled three servants out of the dozens who were working together.

"What did we do? Are we in trouble?" The three servants smoothed their hair and clothes as they made their way into the master's grand house.

When the master came into the room, all three servants dropped to their knees. "I'm going away. While I'm gone, I want you to take care of my money," he said. He clapped his hands and a man appeared with a tray that held eight bags of gold. "Stand up," the master said to the first servant. "Here are five bags of my gold. I'm trusting you with it," he said, shaking the man's hand. "You're next," he said, pulling the second man to his feet. "I'm giving you two bags of gold." Turning to the third man, he said, "This last bag is for you. I want each of you to invest my money. Take care not to lose it." Then the master left.

Right away the first man invested the five bags of gold. Before very long he had doubled the master's money. The second man also went right to work and before the master returned, he had four bags of gold. But, the third man couldn't quite decide what to do with his one bag of gold. Finally, he took it outside, dug a deep hole, and buried it under a bush.

A long time later the master returned home. "Well, what have you done with my money?" he asked.

"I invested the five bags of gold and now I have ten bags," the first servant announced, dropping the gold at his master's feet and backing away.

"Good job. You are a good servant," the master said.

"I invested my two bags and now I have four," the second man said.

"Good job. You are a good servant," the master said.

Do the best with what you've been given

The third servant nervously stepped forward. "Well, I was afraid because you sometimes get very angry. So I buried the gold you gave me and kept it safe!" he said.

"You didn't invest it? You didn't even put it in the bank to earn interest?" The master couldn't believe what he was hearing. "Take the gold from this man and give it to the one who has ten bags. If you don't do the best with what you've been given, then what you do have will be taken away!"

Based on Matthew 25:14-30

Becoming a Man of God
A man of God is a good steward

When the master gave his money to the three servants and told them to take care of it, he didn't mean they should hide it and give him back the very same amount. He wanted them to take what he gave them and do something with it so they could give more back to him. Each of the three servants had a chance to be good stewards . . . that means they had a chance to do something with the master's money. He was pleased with the two who did that, but he wasn't happy with the one who just buried the money and gave him back the very same amount.

God gives each of his children gifts and talents. If he gives a talent for music, he is pleased if that person takes music lessons to become a better musician. Whatever the talent or gift that is given, it's good to learn to be better at doing it and then to share it with other people.

What gifts or talents has God given you? Do you like to sing or play a musical instrument? Are you good at making people laugh, or are you especially kind to others? How can you get better at using your gift?

Dad's Turn

Tell your son how you have worked to develop talents you have. When you were a child taking music lessons or going to sports camps, did you always enjoy that? Help him to see that improving yourself is sometimes work, but the end result is worth it.

Discuss with your son being a good steward with money, too. Tell him how you try to be wise when making purchases. Explain that you look for the best price on an object so that you get the most for your money. Help him understand that being a good steward is why you can't buy everything he wants.

Tell him about someone whose talents you admire—a musician, speaker, artist, athlete. How does that person share their gift with others? Do you think that person has worked hard to develop their gift?

A Verse to Remember

To those who use well what they are given,
even more will be given,
and they will have an abundance.
Matthew 25:29

A Tale of Two Men

"Out of my way. Let me through. Don't you know who I am?" The Pharisee's fancy robes swished as he pushed his way through the crowd of people entering the Temple for prayer time. Most people stepped out of his way; after all, he was a religious leader–a very important man!

On the other hand, a tax collector tried to get through the crowd for his own prayer time. But, no one stepped aside to let him in. "Dishonest cheat," someone said, right out loud. "That guy stole my hard-earned money and called it taxes. Now I barely have enough money to buy food for my kids," another man whispered to a friend.

Inside the Temple, hundreds of people knelt in prayer. The
Pharisee heard the rumble of voices as their prayers were
offered up to God. Instead of kneeling and praying quietly as
the others were doing, the Pharisee stood up tall and began
to pray loudly, "Thank you, God, that I am not a sinner like
other people . . . especially that tax collector over there. I
don't cheat or lie. I fast twice a week and I give money to
your work. O God, you are so lucky to have a friend like me!"

The people praying nearby couldn't believe what the Pharisee was saying. *We are all sinners*, one woman thought. "Everyone does bad things sometimes. Well, God knows his heart better than I do," she sighed, going on with her own prayers. Across the way, the tax collector finally found a spot to pray. When he knelt, all the nearby people moved away. No one wanted to be around him.

Imagine the surprise of the people around him when they heard his whispered prayers, "O God, please forgive my sins. Show mercy to me, O God." He pounded his hands against his chest because he felt sorry for the unkind and dishonest things he had done.

Jesus told this story to show the difference between proud people who don't admit when they do something wrong and people who know they are sinners.

Based on Luke 18:9-14

Becoming a Man of God

A man of God asks forgiveness for his sins

The Pharisee thought he was better than other people. Maybe he even thought that he didn't ever sin. If he really knew the truth, he would have known that all people are sinners and need to ask God's forgiveness. Tax collectors were usually dishonest cheaters who took more money than people actually owed for taxes. Tax collectors didn't have many friends. The people around him must have been surprised to hear this tax collector's prayer because he was sorry for his sins. He knew that he did wrong things and that he needed to ask God's forgiveness. Even though he did wrong things, he was on the right track because he admitted his sins and asked forgiveness.

Do you ever do wrong things? Do you think that some people never do wrong things? Have you asked God's forgiveness for wrong things you have done?

Dad's Turn

Does your son think that you never do anything wrong or never make a mistake? He might have the impression that only children do wrong things and adults have their lives all together. Give him a general example of how adults still struggle with doing wrong things. Help him to understand that the Pharisee's attitude was completely wrong. Everyone sins and needs to ask God's forgiveness.

Pray with your son now. Both of you may want to ask God's forgiveness and for his help to stop doing the same wrong things over and over.

A Verse to Remember

If we claim we have not sinned,
we are calling God a liar and showing
that his word has no place in our hearts.

1 John 1:10

Bird's-Eye View

"**G**et out of my way! Don't you know who I am? Move it!" Zacchaeus tried to muscle his way through the crowd. But no one paid any attention to the little guy. The fact that he was a tax collector didn't help. No one wanted to do anything nice for him, because he cheated people out of their hard-earned money!

"He's coming!" a man called as he ran toward the crowd. "Jesus is coming!" The crowd of people pushed closer to the road. Zacchaeus found himself at the back of the group. He wouldn't be able to see anything except people's backsides. *I've got to do something. I want to see Jesus, too,* Zacchaeus thought. Then, he had an idea. He climbed up the big sycamore tree next to the road and scooted out to the end of a big branch.

Zacchaeus clung to the branch as the crowd around Jesus passed right below him. He had a bird's eye view of the great teacher! When Jesus stopped and looked up at him, Zacchaeus nearly fell off his branch. "Come down, Zacchaeus. I would like to come to your house," Jesus said.

"M-m-my house? He wants to come to my house?" Zacchaeus was amazed. He jumped down from the tree and proudly walked through the crowd of people who hated him.

The little tax collector wanted to be sure that everyone saw that Jesus wanted to come to HIS house. He felt very important. "Ha! The teacher didn't ask to come to any of your houses," he wanted to say right out loud.

"Why is Jesus going with that cheater?" people complained. "He doesn't deserve special attention from Jesus." The little man ignored the nasty comments as he opened the door to his fine house.

Jesus went inside and closed the door. The tax collector listened as Jesus talked about God's love for all people. He talked to Zacchaeus about the way he had been cheating people out of their hard-earned money. When he finished, Zacchaeus quietly said, "I'm sorry for the way I've lived. I promise to pay back the people I've cheated. In fact, I'll pay back four times more than I owe them. And, I'll give half of my money to the poor." Jesus smiled. He knew that Zacchaeus loved God now and would treat people fairly.

Based on Luke 19:1-10

Becoming a Man of God
A man of God makes things right

Zacchaeus was kind of a creep. He cheated people out of the money they worked very hard to earn. They couldn't do anything about it because he worked for the government. That's why Zacchaeus didn't have any friends and no one cared whether or not he could see Jesus. No one would get out of his way.

But, when Jesus taught Zacchaeus about God and how God wanted him to live, Zacchaeus believed him. Then, Zacchaeus's heart changed and he wanted to be kind to other people. He didn't just decide that from that day on, he would be fair. He decided to pay back the people he had cheated—four times more than he had stolen from them. Jesus was pleased with Zacchaeus.

If you have been unkind or unfair with someone, how can you make things right with them?

Dad's Turn

Tell your son about a time when you were treated unfairly or felt you were cheated. How did you feel about the situation? How did you feel about the person who was unfair or who cheated you? If you had been given a chance to do something nice for that person, would you have done it?

Remind your son that people who don't go to church or read the Bible only know about God by the way God's people treat them. If God's people act with fairness, kindness, and love, others will get a little idea of what God is like. If we learn that we have hurt another person, we should make it right, just as Zacchaeus did.

If your son is sometimes selfish or unkind, talk with him about that behavior and gently suggest that he make an effort to treat others better. Pray with him about the way you both treat others.

A Verse to Remember

Dear children,
let us stop just saying we love each other;
let us really show it by our actions.

1 John 3:18

Dirty Coats, Palm Branches, and Noisy Rocks

"Peter, I don't have a good feeling about this," John whispered.

"Relax, will you? We're just doing what Jesus said to do. If he says it's OK, then it's gotta be OK," Peter whispered back. He untied the rope and started to lead the colt down the path.

"HEY YOU! Are you stealing my colt?" The angry man's face was so red that John thought he might have a heart attack. He ran toward them shaking his fist. "Leave my colt alone!" he shouted.

To John's amazement, Peter very calmly answered, "Sir, we're not stealing this colt; the Master needs it." Even more amazing, the man stopped complaining. He nodded his head, quietly turned around, and went into his house. When they took the colt to Jesus, he started to climb onto it. "Wait," Peter cried. Taking off his coat, he spread it on the colt's back. "OK, now." He stepped aside so Jesus could get on the colt.

The disciples walked along behind the colt that Jesus was riding into Jerusalem. Word spread quickly that Jesus was coming and soon crowds of people lined the road. The disciples looked uneasily at each other as cries of "Hosanna! Bless the King who comes in the name of the Lord!" filled the air.

Peter ducked as a palm branch smacked him in the face. *What are these people doing?* he wondered. Looking around, he saw people waving palm branches in front of Jesus. Other people had spread their coats on the ground so the colt was stepping on them. They didn't even want Jesus' clothes to touch the ground.

"Psst, Peter, look over there," John whispered. Peter turned to see a group of Pharisees standing with their arms folded across their chests. These were not happy men. "Tell your followers to be quiet," one of them snapped at Jesus. In one smooth movement, all the disciples turned to look at Jesus. What would he say to the religious leaders?

"Sir," he quietly replied, "if they kept quiet, the stones along the road would burst into cheers." Slowly, the disciples' heads swiveled back to the Pharisees. But, they didn't say another word. Smart guys.

Based on Luke 19:28-40

Becoming a Man of God
A man of God can't help but praise him

What an amazing sight—Jesus riding a donkey down streets lined with people shouting praises, waving palm branches, and spreading their coats on the ground! The people couldn't stop shouting their praises. They couldn't seem to control themselves. They knew that Jesus was someone special.

When the Pharisees told Jesus to make the people be quiet, he knew that the rocks themselves would shout praises, because when God is present, praise just comes naturally. If the people were quiet, then nature itself would praise him!

How do you praise God? Do you sing? Shout praises? Draw pictures for him? Praise God for something right now!

Dad's Turn

What makes you shout with excitement? Do you get excited while watching sports and loudly cheer for your team? Talk with your son about situations where you get excited enough to shout and cheer.

If you have ever had an experience of being filled with praise and adoration for God to the point of not being able to keep silent, tell your son about it. Tell him how you praised God for that experience.

Remind your son that it is important to praise God for the wonderful things he does and not just always ask him to do things for you.

Ask your son what he would like to praise God for today. Help him do so, either through prayer or song, or making a picture of praise to God.

A Verse to Remember

Let everything that lives
sing praises to the LORD!

Psalm 150:6

My Father's House

"Best deals in town! Get your sacrificial birds here! All your temple needs . . . right here!" The shouts could be heard throughout the usually quiet, respectful hush of the temple, offering the best deals and buys "too good to pass up!" The money-hungry salesmen even had signs hanging from the grand marble columns advertising their deals.

When Jesus came to pray in the temple, he couldn't believe what he saw! Pushing his way through the crowds, he got more and more angry at the salesmen who were stealing money from the worshipers. "Poor Jewish people come here to worship God, but these men are over-charging and stealing money from the worshipers. They are trying to get rich by people's worship!"

"This is not the way to treat God's house!" he continued. Walking up to one man's table, Jesus swung his arm across it, brushing coins and papers to the floor.

"Hey, what do you think you are doing?" the man shouted. Jesus ignored him and began pushing over tables and ripping down signs. Arms grabbed at him, trying to stop the destruction, but he kept right on clearing the temple.

"This is God's house—my Father's house—and it is to be a place of prayer. It is not a place for you to make money by cheating people who come to worship God." Jesus worked his way up and down the aisles, turning over table after table, spilling money and scattering people as he went.

When the floor was covered with coins and birds were flapping all over the temple, the money changers took off running, afraid of what this crazy man might do next. But, Jesus was finished; he had made his point. He sat down and people quickly gathered around him. Some sat in awe, some begged for healing, some wanted him to bless their children. Shouts of, "Praise God for the Son of David!" echoed through the temple. The jealous Pharisees stood in a corner and made plans for ways to get rid of Jesus.

Based on Matthew 21:12-17

Becoming a Man of God
A man of God takes a stand against wrong

Jesus didn't like it when people were cheated. He especially didn't like it when the poor people who came to worship God were cheated. He believed that the temple should not be a place where people came to make money; it was God's house where people came to worship. The people who sold animals to be used in sacrifices had started overcharging and cheating the poor people. Jesus had to stop this kind of behavior. He couldn't let it keep happening.

Have you ever seen something happening that you felt was wrong? Did you see people being mistreated, or cheated? Did you see someone being disrespectful of God's house? Did you do anything to stop the wrong behavior?

Dad's Turn

Have you ever gotten involved in a cause against something you felt was wrong? What was it? How did you get involved? What was the outcome? Were you frightened about getting involved? Did it feel good to have a part in changing something?

Talk with your son about the importance of keeping worship pure. It hurts our worship to be more concerned about making money than about serving God and learning more about him. Jesus wanted people everywhere to have the chance to worship God—not just those who could afford the prices the merchants were charging.

Ask your son if there is any "cause" that he would like to take a stand against. Talk about ways he could get involved and take a stand against something unfair or unjust.

A Verse to Remember

Obey me, and I will be your God
and you will be my people.
Only do as I say, and all will be well.
Jeremiah 7:23

Good News Morning

*I*t's hard to keep going when your hope is taken away, thought Mary. *I know I've done the things I'm supposed to do these past few days, but I honestly can't remember much about them.* The sun was just coming up as Mary and two friends walked to the tomb where Jesus was buried. Hope died for Jesus' followers . . . when he died. He had taught them about God and how to live for him. But, then he died, and now some of them wondered if any of what he taught was true.

Even in the middle of their pain, the three women had to do what was right. Their custom said that Jesus' body must be covered with perfumes and oils, or his burial wouldn't be finished. They wanted to do the right thing so they were trudging to the tomb, even though their hearts were numb with pain.

The three women had been friends for years, shared happy times and hard times, but today, none of them knew what to say, so they walked in silence. But then, one of them remembered watching the soldiers roll a big stone over the opening to the tomb. "It took six soldiers to place that stone. How are we going to move it to get into the tomb?" she asked her friends.

"How much more do we have to go through?" her friend answered, dropping her basket of perfumes. "I just don't know how much more I can take," she sighed.

"Come on, we'll figure something out," Mary whispered. Heads bowed, they rounded the last curve in the road before reaching the tomb. Suddenly, the woman in front stopped, and her friends bumped right into her.

"It's . . . gone!" she whispered. "The stone is gone. What does that mean?" They held onto one another as fear rose in their hearts. "What was going on?"

The bravest of the three slowly
approached the open tomb.
Cautiously stepping inside, she
waited for her eyes to adjust to the
darkness. "You're looking for Jesus, but he's not here. He's alive.
He came back to life, just as he told you he would," the angel's
voice announced. Looking around, the woman saw that Jesus
WAS gone. "He's alive! He's alive!" she shouted to her friends.
"He has come back to life just as he said he would! Praise God!"

Based on Mark 16:1-7

Becoming a Man of God
A man of God celebrates

This story is an example of how little Jesus' friends really understood him. He had told them he would come back to life—but that was too hard for them to believe. So, they were all heartbroken and lost when he died. All their hope was gone. These women going to the tomb were just doing what they did for anyone who died. They surely didn't expect that Jesus' body wouldn't be in the tomb. But, when the angel told them that Jesus was alive, they were filled with high-fiving-heart-skipping joy! HE WAS ALIVE! . . . HE IS ALIVE!

Celebrate this today—even if it's not Easter time! Thank God that Jesus is alive! Tell someone this good news!

Dad's Turn

What's the best news you ever received? Why did it make you so happy? How did you celebrate? Who was the first person you shared your happy news with?

Talk with your son about what Jesus' resurrection means to us. In all other religions, the person who was worshiped died . . . and stayed dead. Jesus came back to life (as he said he would), and he is living in heaven, watching over us, taking care of us, and still paying the price for our sins. Someday, he will come back to earth and get all Christians, taking us to heaven to live with him forever! Celebrate!

A Verse to Remember

Forgetting the past and
looking forward to what lies ahead,
I strain to reach the end of the race
and receive the prize for which God,
through Christ Jesus,
is calling us up to heaven.

Philippians 3:13-14

Seeing Is Believing

"He's dead, all right? Just let it go. We saw the soldiers drag his body down from the cross and put him in the tomb. He's dead, so quit talking about some miraculous resurrection." Thomas stomped around the room shouting at his friends, even though they tried to shush him so the Pharisees wouldn't hear their argument.

"Thomas, just listen. Yes, we saw them put Jesus' body in the tomb. He was dead. We're not arguing that. But, the women went out on Sunday to take care of his body . . . and he was gone!" Peter told the story again, but Thomas kept stomping away. Peter grabbed his arm and pulled him back.

"And then the other day, some of us were in this very room. The door was locked, the windows were shut—that's the honest truth. All of a sudden, Jesus was standing here right in front of us! He talked to us. He said that he was sending the Holy Spirit to help us. He said we should forgive people's sins. It's the truth, Thomas!"

Thomas threw up his hands in disgust. "You're crazy! I tell you, HE IS DEAD! I will not believe what you're telling me unless I see him for myself. No, not just see him, I will have to touch the wounds on his body!" Thomas headed for the door; he had heard enough for one day.

About a week later the disciples were together again in that same locked room. Each man was lost in his own thoughts, when a familiar voice broke the silence: "Thomas. Touch the wounds in my hands and side. Believe."

"Jesus, it's really you. You are alive!" Thomas whispered, sliding off his chair and onto his knees.

"You believe because you can see me and touch me," Jesus said. "Think how special those are who haven't seen me but believe anyway."

Based on John 20:19-29

Becoming a Man of God
A man of God has faith

Thomas was one of Jesus' closest friends, one of the disciples who was with him when he healed sick people and brought dead people back to life. Thomas knew that Jesus could do miracles . . . he had seen it with his own eyes. But, he couldn't believe that Jesus was really alive. His faith just wasn't that strong. So, Jesus appeared to Thomas and even let Thomas touch the scars on his hands from when he was nailed to the cross. Jesus was probably happy to do that, but he pointed out how special people are who believe in him without actually seeing and touching him. Having faith means you believe something is—even if you can't see it or touch it.

Would you be like Thomas and actually have to see Jesus before you believed he was alive? Or, would you believe based on the fact that other people had seen him?

Dad's Turn

Are you a "show me" kind of guy who doesn't easily believe things that you haven't seen for yourself? Tell your son about a time when you had to believe something by just having faith—without any physical or practical reason to believe. Was it hard? Were you later glad that you believed? Did this experience make it easier to have faith the next time?

Talk with your son about some examples of things you both believe in, even though you can't see them or explain them, such as the sun coming up every morning, or the stars and moon staying up in the sky. Discuss things you know to be true about God and explain to your son that since he believes those things, he already has some faith.

Ask God to help your faith grow stronger every day.

A Verse to Remember

You love him
even though you have never seen him.
Though you do not see him,
you trust him, and even now you are happy
with a glorious, inexpressible joy.

1 Peter 1:8

Dreaming a Lesson

"Oh wow! I just had the weirdest dream!" Peter came downstairs rubbing the sleep from his eyes. Simon, his _____ waited for Peter to explain. "This big sheet came down _____ the sky, and it was filled with all kinds of foods that we _____ eat. You know, foods that are unclean." Simon looked _____ sed so Peter explained, "It would be a sin to eat them!" _____ imon got it.

"But then, this voice said, 'Eat this!' I said, 'No way!' but the voice said, 'God says it's OK!' What do you think this means?" Peter asked. Simon just shook his head—he didn't have a clue!

At just about the same time, a Roman army officer named Cornelius was having a pretty weird dream of his own.

In Cornelius's dream an angel said, "God has seen your gifts to the poor. He knows you are a kind man. Send your servant to Joppa to find Peter. Have Peter come here and teach you about God." When Cornelius woke up, he did exactly what the angel had told him to do.

Peter was still trying to figure out what his dream meant when Cornelius's three servants knocked on the door. "What do you want?" he asked them.

"Our master is an officer in the Roman army. He wants you to come back with us and teach him about God."

"Well, it's kind of late. Why don't you stay overnight here and we'll go tomorrow," Peter answered.

When Peter got to Cornelius's house, he was surprised to
see that Cornelius had invited many friends and relatives to
hear what he would teach them. "According to Jewish law,
I shouldn't even be here," Peter said right away. "The law
says that a Jew shouldn't come into the house of someone
who isn't Jewish. But, God taught me an important lesson
in a dream the other day. He taught me that when he says
something is OK, then I should believe him. So, if he wants
you to know about him, I shouldn't refuse to teach you, just
because you're not Jewish." Then Peter taught them many
things about God.

Based on Acts 10

Becoming a Man of God

A man of God has an open mind and heart

The Jewish people lived by pretty strict rules stating what they could and could not do. God spoke to Peter in this dream and basically said, "Lighten up!" God loves all people. He wanted Peter to teach about God's love, even to people who weren't Jewish.

Some people today live by pretty strict rules, too. They only want to be around people who think like they do, dress like they do, speak the same language—but if we all felt like that, some people would never hear about God's love!

Do you know any kids who speak a different language than you, or are from another country? Do they have different beliefs or customs? Are you uncomfortable being around them? How can you be friendlier to them?

Dad's Turn

Have you ever encountered prejudice? Was it toward you, or did you observe it toward someone else? How did you feel about it? Did you do anything to stop it or try to change people's attitudes?

As you have grown up have you encountered rigid rules about how to live the Christian life? How did these affect your own Christian growth?

Talk with your son about rules—some are good and are made for our safety and protection. Sometimes rules are made because people are afraid to be around those who are different or are afraid of change.

Talk to your son about people in your neighborhood or town who are not necessarily like you. How can you befriend them? How can you help others to be open to getting to know these people? Remind him that only by becoming their friends will you have chances to share God's love with them.

A Verse to Remember

Love each other.
Just as I have loved you,
you should love each other.

John 13:34

Prison Break!

"Can't you take these chains off so I can sleep?" Peter asked. But, his guards didn't even answer. After all, they were chained to him, so they were going to have trouble sleeping, too. With a guard on each side of him, Peter leaned back against the prison's stone wall. But one guard snored so loudly that neither Peter nor the other guard had any hope of getting any rest. Peter sighed and settled down to watch bugs crawl around the floor.

Why am I in prison anyway? Peter thought. *I didn't do anything except teach people about Jesus. Why is that so bad?* Even as he thought that, Peter remembered his friend, James. King Herod murdered him because of his faith . . . and people laughed and cheered that murder! *I wonder what the king plans to do with me?* Peter was a little nervous. *I've got to get some sleep.* He tried to shake the anxious thoughts from his mind. He rolled the snoring guard onto his side, trying to shut him up. That made the chain cut into his leg, but it was better than the snoring.

It was very late when Peter finally fell asleep. He had nightmares about what might happen to him. Since there were four squads of four soldiers standing guard outside his cell, he knew that King Herod wanted to be sure he didn't escape.

Peter's sleep was restless. He tried to toss and turn, but the chains wouldn't let him. Right in the middle of his nightmare a bright light shone into his cell. It was brighter than anything he had ever seen.

Something stuck him in the ribs, and Peter opened his eyes. "Is it morning already?" he moaned. "Wait a minute; the guards are still sleeping, so I must be dreaming." Then he saw a shining angel standing in front of him.

"Get up and get dressed," the angel said. Peter shook his chained arms. "How am I supposed to move?" he started to ask. But before he could say a word, the chains fell off his arms and legs. The angel motioned for Peter to follow him through the prison, past the sleeping guards, and out the door. Soon Peter was standing on the street outside the prison.

"How can I ever thank . . ." Peter turned to say, but, the angel was gone! Now Peter knew for sure that he wasn't dreaming.

He hurried to see his friends, who were praying for him. At first the servant who answered the door was so shocked that she forgot to open it for him. "Hey, let me in." Peter pounded on the door. When she opened the door, Peter rushed in and told everyone how God had saved him from prison and whatever King Herod had planned for him.

Based on Acts 12:1-19

Becoming a Man of God
A man of God is saved by God

Peter was in jail because he was a Christian—not a very popular thing to be. His only crime was teaching about Jesus. He knew that some other Christians had been put in jail and were not treated very well—James was killed—and the people laughed! We don't know if Peter was frightened or if he came close to giving up hope. However, we do know that God sent the angel to lead him out of prison. God saved Peter from whatever King Herod had planned. Peter trusted God enough to obey the angel and follow it out of prison.

God takes care of his children. He often saves us from problems—not always with a big show like sending an angel, but every day he protects his children from danger or problems.

Thank God for his salvation and protection in your life.

Dad's Turn

Tell your son about a time you were rescued or protected from danger by someone. How did you feel? Were you frightened? Now tell him about ways you have protected him from danger or problems. Tell him you love him and are constantly concerned for his safety and well-being.

Thank God for his love and protection for both of you. Thank God for providing a way of salvation for his children.

A Verse to Remember

The LORD keeps watch over you
as you come and go,
both now and forever.

Psalm 121:8

Carolyn Larsen has written more than thirty books for children and adults. She is a frequent conference speaker around the world, bringing scriptural messages filled with humor and tenderness. She is also active in a theater troupe and cofounded the group Flashpoints, which uses drama and creative movement to minister at women's events.

Caron Turk is an artist whose work has appeared in the bestselling series of Little Boys/Little Girls Storybooks as well as in numerous original paintings, designs, and stamps.

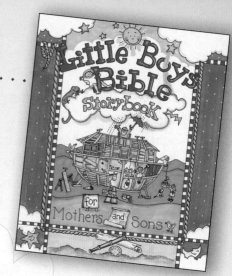
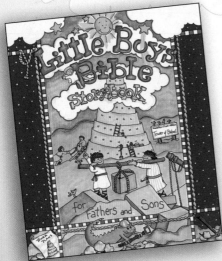

Bible stories for
mothers & **daughters** . . .

In *Little Girls Bible Storybook for Mothers and Daughters*, all stories are uniquely told from a mother's perspective. Includes additional material not found in *Little Girls Bible Storybook*.

. . . and **fathers** & **daughters** to read together.

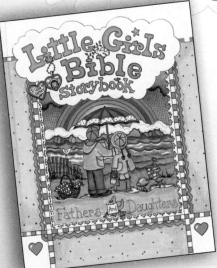

In *Little Girls Bible Storybook for Fathers and Daughters*, all stories are uniquely told from a father's perspective. Includes additional material not found in *Little Girls Bible Storybook*.

BakerBooks
Relevant. Intelligent. Engaging.
www.bakerbooks.com

Now in one collection!

Little Girls Bible Storybook

This updated edition combines the most popular stories from the bestselling *Little Girls Bible Storybook for Mothers and Daughters* and *Little Girls Bible Storybook for Fathers and Daughters*.

BakerBooks

Relevant. Intelligent. Engaging.

www.bakerbooks.com